# DISCOVERING
## *Forgiveness*

# THEOLOGICAL POSTINGS SERIES

Many faithful Christians seek to be informed about current events and apply their faith convictions to our complex and conflicted world. However, most have a hard time finding space in their busy schedules for scholarly inquiry and also experience a great deal of theological writing to be difficult to understand and apply. Many do not need to be convinced to take theology seriously so much as to be provided theological writing that meets them halfway—and provides them with access to the relevance of Christianity's biblical-theological resources.

The concise volumes in the Theological Postings Series seek to meet this need. These books are grounded in solid scholarship but wear it lightly. They connect the biblical narrative and theological tradition with contemporary issues. Thus they provide an "exegesis" of the contemporary situation as well as of the biblical world and of the churches in history.

The Theological Postings Series is currently edited by Ted Grimsrud and C. Norman Kraus and released by Cascadia Publishing House LLC.

1. The Jesus Factor in Justice and Peacemaking
   *C. Norman Kraus, 2011*

2. Discovering Forgiveness:
   Pathways Through Injury, Apology, and Healing
   *Larry Dunn, 2014*

# DISCOVERING
# *Forgiveness*

## Pathways Through
## Injury, Apology, and Healing

### LARRY A. DUNN
**Foreword by *John Paul Lederach***

*Theological Postings Series, Volume 2*

**Cascadia**
**Publishing House**
Telford, Pennsylvania

**Cascadia Publishing House LLC orders, information, reprint permissions:**
*contact@cascadiapublishinghouse.com*
1-215-723-9125
126 Klingerman Road, Telford PA 18969
www.CascadiaPublishingHouse.com

**Library of Congress Cataloguing-in-Publication Data**
Dunn, Larry (Professor)
Discovering forgiveness : pathways through injury, apology, and
healing / by Larry A. Dunn.
  pages cm. -- (Theological postings series ; volume 2)
Includes bibliographical references.
Summary: "Drawing from many fields, this volume provides an
accessible and interdisciplinary approach to understanding the
complexity of forgiveness while generating practical applications."
"[summary]"-- Provided by publisher.
ISBN 978-1-68027-000-6 (5.5 x 8.5 trade pbk. : alk. paper)
1. Forgiveness. I. Title.
BJ1476.D86 2014
158.2--dc23

                    2014037876


20 11 19 18 17 16 15 14     10 9 8 7 6 5 4 3 2 1

*For Seth*
*(1990 - 2011)*
*who lived fully, loved deeply, and forgave freely;*

*and*

*to his mother, Susan, and his brothers, Eli and Isaac.*

# CONTENTS

*Foreword by John Paul Lederach*    11
*Author's Preface*    13
*Acknowledgments*    16
*Introduction*    19

### 1 Discovering Forgiveness  •  25
Understanding Forgiveness
The Power of Metaphor
Forgiveness Is Like
A Tentative Conclusion

### 2 Pathways of Forgiveness  •  38
Many Paths
Beyond Injury
Withdrawal and Reflection
Stuck Along the Path
Extending Grace

### 3 The Power of Forgiveness  •  51
The Power of Apology
The Structure of Apologies

Negotiations
The Dynamics of Power
Beyond Apology

## 4 The Justice of Forgiveness • 68

Conditional and Unconditional
Justice and Memory
Forgive and Forget?
Remember
Beyond Memory
Non-Remembering
Freedom from Memory's Hold

## 5 The Practice of Forgiveness • 84

A Peacemaking Practice
Practising the Practice of Forgiveness
The Doing and Being of Forgiveness
Beyond Practise: The Art of Forgiveness
On Confusion

## 6 Beyond Forgiveness • 97

The Problems of Forgiveness
Simple and Complex
Conclusion

*Notes*   *111*
*The Author*   *122*

# FOREWORD

When approaching forgiveness we all face a certain dilemma. Forgiveness simultaneously is central across faith traditions and yet at times has been taught as obligation bordering on manipulation. With wisdom won from personal experience and years of engaged conflict transformation, Larry Dunn unravels the promise and challenge of forgiveness much as in the fable of the blind folk touching and understanding the many sides of the elephant. This book helps generate a wonderful encounter. The journey we follow takes us into both theological understanding and praxis, attending respectfully to the complexity of forgiveness, to a wonderfully multi-dimensional act of grace.

The title—*Discovering Forgiveness*—provides the very platform that supports the flow of the conversation. *Discover* in Latin suggests gaining sight about that which is unknown, *unveiling* little by little something that has been shrouded.

*Forgiveness* follows a pathway that requires us to step into the unknown. This is not a book that offers us a once-and-it's-over approach or magic wand. As Dunn stresses, forgiveness invites us to live with paradox. We hold at one time, together, multiple experiences and truths that on the surface could easily appear contradictory—yet when embraced permit a deeper, more authentic and vulnerable pathway toward our shared humanity.

In forgiveness, Dunn writes, it's okay to be stuck while finding your way. In forgiveness, memory and grace can live in the same house. Forgiveness can never be forced and obligated, but is always available and tends to rise with unexpected energy and power to shift human relationships toward restoration and healing.

Dunn offers a stream of provocative stories—of real people in honest conversations. For me, these stories create a deep grounding in both the potential and the complexity, the challenges and the actual examples, of how forgiveness emerges and finds expression. At times I found myself feeling profound admiration for the power of love expressed beyond merit, the ways forgiveness always breaks into daily life as unexpected surprise and gift. For example, the humble yet extraordinary act of a musician, betrayed in friendship by a village neighbor who killed his father during the Rwandan genocide, to seek out his old friend, not in revenge but with a new capacity to love and leave hatred behind, amazes me.

At other times I found myself feeling stuck with the young woman caught in a church conflict who was not ready to forgive, squeezed between pressure to offer her blessing yet knowing she had not truly reached that place. I could feel the weight and guilt, the inner fight going on to express her deepest feeling even as she worried what others would think. Maybe I should just do what everyone else seems to ask of me. "Don't," Dunn suggests. Genuine forgiveness rises from authenticity, not dishonesty. Too often in church life we get carried along by pressures to conform—we get "shoulded-on" more than we care to imagine. *Discovering Forgiveness* cleans the slate. Dunn opens space for a deeper and more meaningful conversation about a central tenet and practice of faith.

And here lies the subtle but maybe most significant contribution of this book: You will find yourself in it. You will be drawn into all sides of the paradoxes. You will listen in new and honest ways to your own experience. You will feel the promise, appeal, and provocations forgiveness affords when we seek genuine encounter with self, other, and God.

—*John Paul Lederach, Professor of International Peacebuilding, University of Notre Dame*

# Author's Preface

A growing number of publishers have established a series of books in peacemaking and conflict studies. The best volumes, in my opinion, are those which are academically sound but accessible to the non-scholarly reader. They are helpful not only because they present well-researched ideas (theory) to those less likely to avail themselves of more scholarly works (practitioners) but also because they recognize that students and even scholars want clear, readable, and comprehensible volumes on topics of interest. Before I knew that Cascadia would be my publisher, I set out to produce a book of this kind whether part of such a series or not. That is one objective of this book.

At one point in the development of peace-focused series entries, I noted a surprising and obvious gap in the selected topics: no works on forgiveness. I sensed a need for such a volume among both scholars and practitioners and developed an interest in bringing together some twenty-five years of experience and exposure to a variety of perspectives I had encountered during that time. Thus I set out to put my own thoughts on the subject into a single volume. To paraphrase Frederick Buechner, I saw this as a small way to fulfill my calling to peace education by finding a place to have one of the world's greatest needs come together with my own deep passion.

A key element of my passion is theological. As a follower of Jesus for more than three decades, I have always felt both inspired and challenged by his example and call to peace, justice, reconciliation, and healing. My membership in the Anabaptist faith community was originally and continues to be an affirmation of my commitment to such ideals and practices by my adopted religious tradition, and vice versa. Though my interest led me to a degree in theology at Fuller Theological Seminary, I am no theologian, nor is this a theological volume *per se*. Nevertheless, although not all of my peacemaking work, nor that of my students, is rooted in a particular religious or theological context, whether explicit or not, I have felt it important as a follower of the Prince of Peace to integrate my faith theologically with my identified academic discipline and here with forgiveness in particular.

Thus, narratives such as the Genesis (37-50) account of Joseph and his brothers, the Forgiving Father (Luke 15:11-32, typically referred to as the Prodigal Son), and various aspects of the Sermon on the Mount (Matt. 5-7) offer insight and guidance to the other disciplinary perspectives on conflict and forgiveness, even if not explored explicitly or in significant detail here.

It is particularly satisfying when, in the course of the integration enterprise, one discovers empirical support from the social sciences, for example, for a principle highlighted in these ancient narratives. And still more is to be gained from actual theologians who have worked hard to expand our understanding of such matters. All that to say that I have allowed this work to be theologically informed in the broadest sense of that word, providing both motivation and insight.

As a way of assuring the reader that the feet of this work are planted firmly on the ground, let me note the hope that this book will have practical significance. I hope it will make a difference for those who themselves journey or walk with others in situations where forgiveness is needed or desired.

This is important for me because I have found myself in such settings over the last twenty-five years. While serving with the Mennonite Central Committee in Labrador, Canada, I had the enormous privilege of working with people in Aboriginal communities whose very identities were under threat. Historically, these were people who were relocated and suffered all manner of oppression and abuse—not a prime context for forgiveness. Once a community leader, having been asked by the church for forgiveness of past abuses, simply refused to extend it. And I'll never forget returning to the United States to news that a young man from a village I had worked with closely had committed suicide. He had been unable to find freedom from his fear that he might abuse own son as he had been abused when growing up.

These were the kind of realities that opened my eyes to the challenges of forgiveness. But I also knew the Aboriginal communities there to be forgiving of their own and of others (including me from time to time) out of concern for the healing they knew was integral to their survival no matter the threat. One cannot write a book about forgiveness without constantly holding it up to such experiences and demanding that it wrestle with the reality of the challenges they present.

The reception this work has had even before publication undergirds my hopes for it. Within my network of colleagues, friends, members of my faith community, practitioners and other peacemakers, awareness of my work on this book has led to numerous opportunities to present what I have been learning. Though I wish it were true, because the book has not yet been available I cannot rightly claim that its insight or popularity was the source of this interest. However, it does testify to broad interest, widespread curiosity, and deeply felt need related to forgiveness.

This has very little to do with the existence of books on the subject and virtually everything to do with the almost daily human experience of life as filled with painful and unresolved conflict. I know this to be true in my own life. I have also been humbled by those who have shared the challenges and pain of their experience as they have invited me to discuss what I've come to learn about our collective journey down the pathways through injury, apology, and healing.

—*Larry A. Dunn*
  *Fresno, California*

# ACKNOWLEDGMENTS

I have a challenging but extremely rewarding job as a professor. And while it is a hope, if not an expectation, that someone in my position will produce a book as part of that work, it was not clear to me that it would ever come to fruition. It has and as a result there are many people to thank.

I am first grateful to Fresno Pacific University for providing me with a sabbatical that freed me from regular teaching and other duties and created the space to begin such an endeavor. While it took much time beyond my official sabbatical to complete, I accomplished the bulk of my writing during that initial semester. Later my dean, Kevin Reimer, and provost, Steve Varvis, released me from an additional course to allow me some final time to finish.

My program colleagues at the Center for Peacemaking and Conflict studies, Ron Claassen, Dalton Reimer, Duane Ruth-Heffelbower, Jill Schellenberg, and Peter Smith, along with other university colleagues, including Bret Kincaid, Tim Geddert, Rod Janzen, Tim Neufeld, and Laura Roberts, offered encouragement and opportunities for interaction about my subject. I hope they, and the entire FPU community, will see this as a modest contribution to scholarship by a member of faculty.

I'm also grateful for the receptivity, encouragement, direction, and guidance of my publisher, Michael A. King, in support of this volume as a Cascadia Publishing House resource. As it turned out, when I was searching for a publisher and thought of Cascadia, I did so remembering that Michael had been my pastor more years ago than either of us care to admit at Germantown Mennonite Church in Philadelphia. And, as far as I can tell, while Michael was appropriately and carefully professional in not allowing that personal connection to influence his scrutiny of my proposal and manuscript, I appreciate the pastoral care he offered through what can be a difficult process as I encountered challenges along the way.

I am also thankful for the careful reading and critical feedback that Ted Grimsrud and Norman Kraus offered as part of their consideration of this volume for Cascadia's Theological Postings Series, of which they are editors by arrangement with Cascadia. Whether or not it would eventually be adopted as part of that series (as I'm pleased that ultimately it was), I knew their experienced eyes and invaluable suggestions would make this a much better volume.

Outside of Cascadia, I appreciated Tim Nightingale's interest in my manuscript, his careful reading of it, and suggestions that helped me develop and add clarity to several sections. Lastly, mentor and friend David Augsburger offered his usual unqualified and enthusiastic support and encouragement of this project. I knew that it would be a mistake to ignore his gracious admonition to simply "send it off" instead of taking some extra time to address his helpful suggestions. I was able to give attention to one of his key ideas in the time that I had available and only then took his advice.

Finally, in the course of such projects life happens. It's what can make them take much longer than anticipated. But that small sacrifice is worthwhile when the stuff of life involves family and friends. That became unmistakably clear when during the course of this project I lost my son Seth. It is to him, along with his mother Susan and our sons Eli and Isaac, that this book is dedicated.

Because of that tragic event, I went more than a year in the middle of this project without writing a word. Grieving made that, among many other things, impossible. At some point along the way I came across the proverb that there are three things that we should do before we die: write a book, raise a child, and plant a tree. I suppose that each of these, and their collective attainment, suggests something about a life well-lived, without saying anything about their relative importance to one another. As a friend suggested, the only conclusion one can come to about the loss of a child is that it is an awful way to learn so little. I have learned so much more from Seth's life than from his death.

And though they are now both away at school on their own, I am happy for still having a bit more raising to do with my other sons. I will be forever grateful to them, along with my wife Susan, for making possible less important things like book writing. And there is a small tree, a pink Crepe Myrtle donated by my colleagues, in our front yard in Seth's memory.

# INTRODUCTION

Forgiveness, it seems, is a topic about which many have thought deeply and many more have written![1] The real-life challenges of forgiveness can be found daily in the news media and represented in other creative formats as well. Hardly a season goes by without another new book or movie taking up this complex topic, revealing the desperate human search for healing of self and relationships in conflict. A simple Internet search yields literally millions of results leading to countless forums, campaigns, projects, and other resources for exploring the many dimensions of forgiveness. An "app" available for my cell phone even offers up a treasure trove of daily forgiveness quotes!

What can be found there and elsewhere reflects a wide array of understandings about, and experiences of, forgiveness. Some of these provide profound insight and undoubtedly help many along their own path from injury to healing.

But I wonder if the complementary, and at times contradictory, principles and processes, steps and stages, descriptions and prescriptions offered also contribute to our inability to find true forgiveness. A new model encourages us to try again. Another story inspires us to help others struggling to make amends. A simplistic concept or idiom falls short of our painful reality. We try harder and harder to achieve the right attitude and may even say the "magic" words—"I'm sorry," "I forgive you"—only to find ourselves filled with anxiety, guilt and shame, unable to let go of resentment, bitterness, rage.[2]

From this we realize that forgiveness can be made to seem too simple. But is it so complex that we dare not even try? And how is it that even as interest in the topic of forgiveness seems to be expanding, its practice, as L. Gregory Jones suggests, is increasingly undermined, marginalized, and trivialized as exceptional and isolated acts?[3]

The risk of being included among those who have merely added words without providing additional insight comes with any attempt to make a complex topic more understandable. However, to keep from writing on important topics because of that difficult challenge in no way guarantees that those less qualified will show similar restraint. As an academic, my skepticism about the value of such efforts and reluctance to contribute to this topic of wide and increasing interest was overcome when I came across the following commentary from Ron Sider, an author well known for making the complex issues of economics and theology both accessible and understandable.[4] He argues that more scholars need to "popularize" ideas that would otherwise remain in ivory towers, or worse:

> ... some scholars must do it. Plato said that if the wise disdain the task of politics, then they must suffer being governed by fools. Somebody will write popularizing books for "the average person." If those with scholarly training will not do it, they should not complain when those with little expertise do it badly, embarrass the church, and mislead laypeople with one-sided, simplistic nonsense.[5]

Forgiveness is a topic of much interest and people will go on writing about it, sometimes badly in uninformed, simplistic, and even misleading ways. However, I don't want to be overly dismissive or overly critical—there is often something to be gained from almost every understanding of forgiveness; at least that's what I hope to show here in my approach. Other more lengthy scholarly works address the range of forgiveness topics in far more depth than I will attempt here. There is a place for nearly every perspective, and the questions to address about forgiveness are many:

- What makes forgiveness possible?
- How can you forgive those who don't know or acknowledge the harm they've caused? As the victim, why is that burden too on me?
- What if I don't want to forgive or be forgiven? What if I'm not ready?
- Is forgiveness something you do for yourself, or someone else?
- Do our emotions lead us to, or follow, a decision to forgive? Where do my values and beliefs fit in?
- Is forgiveness only a religious idea? An individual therapeutic process? Or something more?
- Forgive and forget? Or, forgive and remember?
- How can one become more forgiving, in a healthy way?
- Must forgiveness lead to reconciliation?

The purpose of this short work is to examine some of the key aspects of forgiveness—from injury to apology and healing—raised by these and other questions about our understanding and practice of it. I propose to do that by exploring the insights provided by some of the many metaphors of forgiveness discovered across a range of approaches examining the ideas and practices of forgiveness.

As someone trained in both the social sciences and theology, my interests are many, and I seek to draw from a wide and rich array of available resources, including numerous scholarly disciplines. With respect to theology, my Anabaptist professional context, involvement in a believers church community, and personal faith commitments not only contribute to my thinking but provide a significant, if not exclusive, audience for which I write.

However, I may need to ask for special allowance from that group and those within other traditions. I'm afraid that my Christian readers may not find this work biblical or theological enough for their liking and perhaps others will find it too much so. I hope that the former can nevertheless see merit in the book as a Christianly resource for faith and life and that the latter can feel I've sufficiently honored different perspectives through a diverse and inclusive approach.

My hope is that this book will be helpful to those involved in all forms of peacemaking where people who struggle with forgiveness are encountered. The demands of their efforts and of the people with whom they work don't always allow for the luxury afforded to those of us with at least one foot in the academic world to become familiar with the vast research and writing that must be sifted through to find the most helpful insights and further develop some of our own.

My past experience and ongoing work as a peacemaking practitioner, in a wide variety of conflict settings, helps with that process. What I can do here, however briefly, will hopefully provide some guidance to those already journeying down their own path.

# DISCOVERING
# *Forgiveness*

*Chapter 1*

# DISCOVERING FORGIVENESS

In the northernmost region of Labrador (Canada), I worked on occasion in an Inuit village facing various forms of violence and conflict that had become increasingly disruptive to community life. This remote setting was not insulated from serious problems of neglect that all too frequently led to myriad forms of abuse, injustice, and oppression, both from within and without.

The community had tried various approaches to dealing with such issues over the years, but none had addressed the the deeper problems, and a disproportionately large Royal Canadian Mounted Police (RCMP) station managed to keep its staff busy. Community members courageously struggled to overcome incidents of substance abuse and domestic violence as well as the wrongs of corporate and governmental manipulation. These experiences left the village, and others like it in the region, much in need of healing, forgiveness, and reconciliation. When made possible through the determined efforts of village leaders, such outcomes were as beautiful as the wide-open Labrador landscape that was home to these native peoples.

But these problems, and their history, were complex and not easily overcome. One such effort exemplified that challenge. In September 2000 an unprecedented gathering of representatives of four different church denominations met in

St. John's, Newfoundland, to apologize to native peoples for their role in 500 years of suffering since Europeans arrived. One by one, the leaders of the Mi'ˆkmaq, Metís, and Inuit stepped forward to accept the apology. However, Peter Penashue, leader of the Innu Nation, stood alone in dissent.

"Let me first of all say that I have the greatest respect for these men who have organized this conference," he began.

> But I must say that I cannot accept the apology. I cannot accept the apology because I don't know what you're apologizing for. Are you apologizing for the time a 10 year-old boy [was sexually abused by the priest] only to go home to be slapped by his mother across the face, and to be told, "Don't you ever say anything bad about these priests. They are men of god"? I don't know if you understand what it is that we've experienced.[6]

Forgiveness can take many forms, shaped individually and culturally by a broad spectrum of centrally held values.[7] We have seen leaders demand, present, and accept forgiveness on behalf of entire peoples, sometimes over centuries of collective wrongdoing as part of complex, negotiated agreements.[8] For others, as in the example of the Labrador Innu described above, forgiveness is more difficult. Yet we also see instances of forgiveness freely given and received such as when children purely, unconditionally, and quickly move from offense to renewed trust.

Forgiveness has many facets and is part of many different experiences and processes. The injury virtually inevitable in all human relationships is no doubt its least desirable aspect, but without it there would be no need for forgiveness. Subtle shifts in power between victim and offender influence decisions to offer or accept an apology, pursue or reject opportunities for reconciliation. We may think of forgiveness, on the one hand, as the ideal outcome to conflict, an almost superhuman response to injury; or, on the other hand, as a real risk to our fragile, vulnerable selves.

Whether understood as an unfolding internal process or a decisive, other-directed act, the unexpected power of forgiveness draws us to real accounts of almost unimaginable human tragedy unforeseeably transformed into stories of genuine healing and long-lasting peace. For every act of inhumanity there are alternative accounts of grace and mercy that attest to the human capacity to forgive and be forgiven, even for that which is—or at least seems—unforgivable.

## UNDERSTANDING FORGIVENESS

But what is forgiveness? To some it may seem simple, straightforward . . . merely another type of human transaction. To others, forgiveness may seem an impossibility that exceeds human capacity, given the issues raised, the complexity of persons, the countless situations, circumstances, and considerations that must be made for its realization. Consider the following composites of real cases:

> The family of a promising, young professional athlete find it within themselves to forgive the teammate responsible for his death, knowing he too will have to live with the mistake the rest of his life. They come alongside their lost son's friend, even though their baffling choice to offer support to this offender puts them at odds with an ambitious prosecutor intent on making an example of a public figure.

> A mother struggles to forgive those who dishonor her son's memory as a courageous public servant. An emergency responder to the tragic events of 9-11, his unrecovered remains are eventually removed from ground zero and lost in a landfill with tons of other debris. She is stuck, unable first to forgive herself for a breach in their relationship no longer reparable after her son's death.

> A young female victim-survivor desperately seeks the recognition of the harm caused by her brother's sexual abuse. But, she wonders, as an adolescent was he even aware of the harm being done? Was he too being abused by someone else? Her uncertainty, and

the risk of pushing him away and losing any chance for reconciliation between them prevents her granting him the forgiveness she needs for her own healing.

A black South African community worker confronts a member of the security police in a Truth and Reconciliation Commission hearing. Detained and punished without trial, he offers forgiveness to an apartheid official seeking amnesty for his role in those beatings and for killing another family member. He recognizes not only his own scars but those of his perpetrators and what is needed to help an entire country recover from its violent past. "They need us," he explains, "to help them regain their own humanity."

Upon being released from prison, a once-violent man convicted of the murder of a female student is hired by the non-profit organization her parents founded. Dedicated to providing alternatives to gangs, he now guides at-risk youth away from the unending, escalating spiral of violence that he managed to escape only through their incomprehensible act of forgiveness.

These only begin to illustrate the many and varied instances of offense, violation, and brokenness in human relationships that may give rise to expressions of forgiveness. Several of the examples represent more exceptional responses of individuals caught up in larger global events, including wars and acts of terrorism. Sadly, others reflect the too familiar and too-common struggles of regular persons within everyday incidents of wrongdoing, harm, and victimization.

Further study only reinforces the difficulty of ever fully understanding forgiveness, despite the fact that it is examined ever more scientifically using the latest technology for identifying the neurobiological bases for human response patterns. One of the challenges in understanding forgiveness comes in defining forgiveness. There seems to be more agreement on what it is not than what it is. We are admonished that forgiveness is not about glossing over wrongs. Forgiveness is not amnesia. Forgiveness is not pardoning, condoning, or excusing; forgiveness does not remove consequences. Forgiveness does not have to include reconciliation; forgiveness is not the same as accepting, tolerating, trusting. Forgiveness is not a magic trick, and so forth. Each of these points, consistently made by various authors and practitioners, seems primarily intended to address the problems and concerns that stand in the way of forgiveness, something we will address more directly later.

Defining forgiveness is also made difficult because it touches so many aspects of our lives: moral, ethical, spiritual, psychological, legal, theological, and so on. While careful descriptions of what one means by forgiveness can be helpful for calling attention to the assumptions that guide one's work, the many issues raised in each of these realms cannot simply be addressed by definitions alone, and certainly not by a single definition.[9]

In any case, different meanings of forgiveness don't necessarily present us with a problem. It may be better to think in terms of understandings of forgiveness than of a particular (and singular) understanding. So I also won't offer another new definition here but will strive instead for an understanding that emerges from a different kind of approach.

One alternative to using definitions is to explore the metaphors we associate with a particular experience, topic, or idea.[10] I have seen this have a powerful effect in places where academics are rightly questioned about how relevant their definitions and understandings are for a particular setting.

## THE POWER OF METAPHOR

Several years before I began working in Labrador, the Labrador Inuit Association (LIA) had sent a contingent of community leaders to New Zealand to learn about how Family Group Conferences, which had been used so successfully among the Maori population, might help them in their own aboriginal context deal with issues of community justice. For whatever reasons, that and other programs had not continued successfully.

Thus the Inuit had good reason to be skeptical of more outside "help" in the form of my involvement. I was keenly aware that I might not be viewed much differently, even though I worked with a respected organization that had been in the community for over forty years and had been invited by village leaders to help them think about the problems of conflict and violence.

I arrived to help conduct a workshop in early May, and snow still covered the ground in this small village where it is winter eight months of the year. In working closely with the leaders, we had planned to emphasize my "facilitative" role in a community workshop rather than that of outside expert. As people gathered in a large room I became increasingly anxious about how many people had showed up and what expectations they might have of our time together. After being introduced, I led them in an exercise designed to get everyone thinking about our focus for the day.

We distributed paper and things with which they could draw and color. Instead of beginning with some definitions on an overhead up front, I asked them to think about how they would complete the following sentence: "Community conflict in our village is like...."[11] Rather than answering the question aloud, I invited each person to draw a picture or image of what came to mind.

As people began to work on their own, an elder that I had noticed standing quietly near the door now spoke up. I didn't recognize him from our planning meetings, and one of the other elders with whom I had been working told me later that he had refused to participate.

"Why are you wasting our time with drawing?" he asked. "The problems we face in our community are serious, and we don't have time for such things."

I acknowledged his concern and was grateful when a community leader stepped forward and asked him if we could just continue and see where the day led us. The elder again said that he thought it would be a waste of our time but allowed us to proceed and returned to his spot by the door in the corner of the room.

I refocused on our activity and the group was ready to share. After several humorous drawings and insightful examples, I asked if there was one more person who wanted to speak. A woman stood and held up her page for all to see. It was a picture of a small flower on the white background of the paper.

"To me," she said, "the community problems in our village are like the long, harsh winter. But we must learn to deal with them because our children are like this precious little flower trying to break through the hard snow of spring. If we don't take care of them, they will be trampled or run over and the pain in our community will become even greater."

The group was silent in response to these powerful words. I could barely continue and was grateful that we had scheduled a break right after the exercise which we then moved into. Everyone seemed to be reflecting on what she had shared. But my own thoughts were interrupted by the sight of the elder who had spoken making his way up front. He came right up to me, and I prepared myself for what he might say.

"This is the most important thing that we have done in our community in a long time," he said. "She is right," he added, nodding toward the woman who had last spoken. "If this helps us find a way to care for our children, then it will have been worthwhile."

Since then, the entire village has moved from their old location to a new site, and I can't say for sure what role, if any, that workshop had in improving community life. But that day I saw how a simple image had a transforming effect on an entire group's understanding of what was important about their life together in a way that no definition could ever have done.

## FORGIVENESS IS LIKE . . .

This story from my experience in Labrador illustrates how metaphors can expand our understanding of something beyond a more "rational" or academic approach. Metaphors can provide insight into how we make sense of the world by revealing to us the meaning, values, assumptions, feelings, and more connected to a lesser known or analyzed aspect of our life by—sometimes surprisingly—comparing it to something well known.

Seeing the human experience of injury and forgiveness as like something that occurs on a pathway (to identify a central metaphor of this book's title) provides insight into forgiveness as a process—as opposed to a one-time event in which something unknown may be discovered along the way. This helps us realize there are times when we might best be able to forgive only after we grant ourselves permission to stop trying at that particular point and move on with other parts of our journey. We may then become unstuck once we see we are stuck not despite—but because of—our efforts.

Anticipating forgiveness as something that might lead to reconciliation helps us to see it not as an unachievable ideal of the morally superior but as the unexpected possibility and unforeseen reality of grace. This is not the scientific perspective that must see to believe. Rather, it is more like something that must first be believed to be seen. Such belief is made possible only through a tenacious hope, one of the most important characteristics of any peacemaker. At times it is only through what can seem like senseless hope that one can persist in working through the seeming impossibility of a violent act or intractable conflict. Yet against all hopelessness, thousands of peacemakers around the world do just that every day.

As suggested above, this acknowledges a certain mystery about forgiveness. I don't use "mystery" here to represent everything that is unexplainable about forgiveness, beyond what we can understand. That can be a kind of irrational rationality! Rather, on this side of the complexity that we recognize, I mean the (metaphorical) mystery that still remains within everything we understand about forgiveness.

Sociologists remind us that we can see and know all the variables of a situation and their relationship to one another and still not be certain about why or how something happened.

One way of measuring our understanding of things is by how well we can quantify them. But that is only one way. As Albert Einstein said, "Not everything that counts can be counted and not everything that can be counted counts." The preeminent twentieth-century scientist was of course making the point that the quality of something is not only or even best measured by that which can be quantified about it. Things like love and beauty, and perhaps also peace and forgiveness, must be measured differently, if their mystery can be "measured" at all.

Our tendency to quantify also reflects the Western belief that the best way to legitimate an idea or practice is to have it somehow be recognized as "scientific," another way of understanding forgiveness. This notion is emphasized in the emerging academic field of forgiveness studies, and there are clearly things to be learned about our experience and understanding of forgiveness through a more rational scientific approach. I'm not suggesting we choose one way of understanding over another. All understandings are necessarily limited, and we should not claim something different about our own. The insight gained by this approach is informing us both about the internal processes of forgiveness and its significance.

A metaphorical approach to understanding forgiveness invites us to see value in ambiguity, paradox, and even contradiction not always embraced by the more rationalistic forms of science. Each approach contributes, complements, expands our understanding beyond the limits of the other.

But certain understandings of forgiveness (or anything) may only seem ambiguous or contradictory because of the limits of our chosen metaphors. For example, we think of a pathway as leading from one place to another. The metaphor makes it difficult to escape the notion of forgiveness as having identifiable, mostly linear steps or stages. Or, in providing us with an image of embrace that reflects the best of the human spirit, even the notion of reconciliation can be treated as if it is the mother and not the child of forgiveness, to draw on yet another metaphor.

Still, consideration of these and other images "gives birth" to the possibility of additional insight. So I want to conclude this first chapter with an exercise that engages a metaphor of a slightly different kind.

### . . . A SOUND

What if we tried to understand forgiveness like a kind of wave of sound or water?[12] Such an image engages us in the physical, temporal, and spiritual characteristics of forgiveness as a part of our life experience. That life experience is like the wave going out from the central point of our being. An injury can be like a disturbance in the water, sending waves of pain through and out from our lives. A wave does not only go out in one direction. A pebble dropped in a quiet lake sends ripples out in circles emanating from the center in all directions. A sound made in the middle of an enclosed space goes out from its source, bouncing back from any encountered object. If continuous, the sound waves going out meet those coming back, changing the hearer's perception.

We can think of this phenomenon as offering a kind of corrective to our tendency to think of forgiveness as following a linear progression or being realized at a single moment in time. Like a sound wave coming back at us, what happens in our past continues to ring true in the present and has an effect on our future. Our experience of injury, apology, forgiveness, reconciliation—with this person now and others before or since, by ourselves or with others in our community—reveals the way in which past, present, and future are simultaneously present and available to us. Forgiveness remembers. Forgiveness is present. Forgiveness expects.

I'm reminded of the way in which a song[13] from our past can take us back to the events and feelings and sense of self for a particular time in which that song was first heard. This is not done by somehow transporting us back in time away from the present. If a particular song evokes a painful memory from the past, it may allow the healing pain of a prior incident to come forward into the present in ways not recently felt. As we hear it, we are still in the present of our current experiences and emotions and identities; we have this sense of nostalgia in our immediate circumstances, perhaps recalling the past exactly as experienced or thinking of it now in a completely different way; even leading to thoughts of the future, anticipating the meaning this song and the experience associated with it might have for us at that time.

Within this metaphor, we might say that the experience of injury and healing that are a part of forgiveness are "echoes" of one another. We hear the forgiving words of our self or the other while we still feel the pain of the past. The genuinely felt healing needed to offer forgiveness in the present occurs while the sound of an apology—recent or long ago—still reverberates in our heart, though, like the ringing in our ears from the loud music of a concert, it gradually fades. The sensed or clearly stated hope of a reconciled future makes possible an act of grace.[14] Waves of pain from the past and healing in the present encounter one another simultaneously, each giving meaning to the other.[15]

This is how remembering not only protects the injured self but also assures the offender that the costly grace being offered is informed by the memory of injury's painful wound and not simply a cheap grace of forgetfulness. This is how recalling the harmful acts of a callous offender not only calls him or her to full accountability but reminds us deep within ourselves of our own human imperfection of the past and present. This is how pursuing forgiveness not only makes possible the releasing of our selves from the trauma of the past but opens the door for the possibility of healing and reconciliation for the future.

Look again at that last paragraph. Perhaps something about it seemed strange to you. If you read it again, replacing "This is how . . ." with "This is why . . .," it might seem to make more sense. Try it. But saying "This is why" instead of "This is how" points us again to the more limiting reasoning and rationale of logical definitions, linear cause and effect. Saying "This is how" points us to an understanding of the many ways forgiveness works in our lives, as revealed in images and metaphors, free from the certainty of one way, one cause, or one reason that so often limits both our understanding and experience. "This is how" also frees us from the imperative implied by "This is why" you must do this and do it in this particular way. This is why you must apologize. This is why you must forgive. This is why you must reconcile. This is why you must remember.

Alternately, "This is how" says, This is one way that leads to the possibility of forgiveness. One path among many. There may be other paths that you might seek. Like studying a biblical text. Like a father who embraces his son. Forgiveness as a journey, with sights and smells and even sounds.

## A TENTATIVE CONCLUSION

Perhaps all forgiveness is impossible, even mad, and not only in its "pure" or unconditional form. Does anyone really deserve forgiveness? Does anyone have the right to ask a victim to find within him or her self the very moral character and decency that is revealed as lacking in their own behavior?

Not all questions are answered, or yet even raised. Perhaps as you've been reading, more questions have come to mind. The question of memory and forgetting. The relationship of forgiveness to reconciliation. We might rightfully ask whether we can, may, or even should forgive the most heinous acts. And in this brief introduction, we have uncovered what may be the most difficult challenge of forgiveness: the definition problem.[16] We are no closer now to a definition of forgiveness than when we began.

However, we have begun to explore some metaphors of forgiveness. Perhaps additional images have come to mind, ripe with insight into the many complex dynamics and possible meanings of forgiveness. In the next chapters we will go more deeply into several key metaphors we've identified here along with others. We'll look at forgiveness as an attitude, a decision, a discovery. A gift, a process, a word. An idea, an action, an interaction. The many aspects of forgiveness, and our ways of thinking about it, are almost endless. Before we're done, we'll consider forgiveness as a kind of practice, and beyond that as a way of both doing and being.

Now let's continue our journey in the next chapter by considering the many paths to forgiveness.

*Chapter 2*

# PATHWAYS OF FORGIVENESS

There are many pathways to forgiveness. In this chapter I want to draw upon the path metaphor, and others connected to it, to reflect on some key elements of the processes leading from injury to forgiveness. The path metaphor affirms the human journey we are on, with our experience of injury and forgiveness as "like all others, like some others, and like no other . . . universally similar, culturally distinct, and individually unique."[17] It invites us to think about (and affirm our experience of) forgiveness as an emerging, circular, interactive, complex process. Consider, for example, the different paths to forgiveness depicted in the following stories.

In October 2006, Charles Roberts carried out a calculated but irrational act of misdirected vengeance born out of unresolved anger that has become an all too familiar part of the American landscape of violence. This time the innocent victims were five Amish school girls of southeastern Pennsylvania's bucolic Bart Township. The blood was barely dry on the floor of the Nickel Mines School when members of the Amish community offered comfort and extended forgiveness to the family of the man who had executed their children and then taken his own life.

Like anyone else, they experienced shock and grief and anger at the tragedy, but they nurtured no sense of malice nor any inclination toward revenge or retaliation. In the days after the murders, some thirty Amish attended Roberts' funeral and even established a charitable fund for the family of the shooter. Many questioned such immediate and total forgiveness, but to do anything other was incomprehensible to the Amish for whom such beliefs and practices are woven into the very fabric of their culture and identity.[18] Several stories from additional contexts:

> Prior to the April 1994 Rwandan genocide, musician Jean Paul Samputu lived with his Tutsi family alongside his Hutu neighbors as trusted members of their community. Warned to leave as tension grew because of his recognition as a rising artist, Jean Paul learned of his family's death while traveling in Burundi and Uganda. All three brothers, a sister, and both parents had been killed, his father by Jean Paul's best friend Vincent.
>
> Shocked by this unthinkable horror, Jean Paul responded with anger, bitterness, alcohol, and thoughts of revenge. After nearly destroying his own life and inspired by his faith, Jean Paul suddenly came to realize that his own healing and renewed capacity to love meant leaving hatred behind. This inspired new songs for sharing what he called a "most unpopular weapon—forgiveness."
>
> Years later Jean Paul returned to Rwanda and learned that Vincent had been released from prison. He went to his village to speak at the *gacaca*, a traditional court, saying that he was there not to accuse Vincent but to "forgive him and set myself free." Unknown to Jean Paul, Vincent was present at the community gathering and stepped out from the crowd, the two of them meeting for the first time since the genocide and the murders. Vincent was shocked by the offer of forgiveness. They shared a meal and over time shared one another's stories, pain, and healing."[19]

In Anne Tyler's novel *Saint Maybe*, Ian Bedloe is a college freshman with a terrible burden. Ian had told his brother Danny that Danny's wife had been cheating on him. Distraught over the news and his unsuspecting naivete, Danny drives his car into a wall, killing himself and leaving a wife and three children. Ian is crushed with overwhelming guilt when, months later, Danny's widow Lucy dies of an overdose of sleeping pills and he gradually comes to suspect that his original accusation of her unfaithfulness may not have been true.

On break from college, a wandering Ian finds himself drawn to the light of a storefront church. Inside he confesses what he's done to Reverend Emmett, looking for reassurance of forgiveness. Ian thinks he hears the reverend incorrectly when he says that, despite his deep sorrow, he is most certainly not forgiven. Even a loving, all-forgiving God can't simply accept an "I'm sorry" without reparation, he's told.

Ian asks how one goes about fixing what can't be undone. Emmett's answer shocks the nineteen year-old college freshman: drop out of college, change his plans, and raise those three orphaned children. Ian can hardly believe this. What kind of God . . . what kind of "cock-eyed religion" would expect such a thing? he wonders. Reverend Emmett's answer is clear: The religion of complete forgiveness . . . what he calls The Religion of the Second Chance.[20]

## Many Paths

The path metaphor provides helpful insights into the dynamics of forgiveness. It first diminishes the notion that forgiveness is exclusively or even primarily a one-time act, something that either happens or doesn't at a given opportunity. Relatively few things instantly or singularly affect us in such major ways in our lives. Beliefs and values are a long time in forming (and re-forming). Often factors we see as immediately effective we eventually understand to be tied directly or indirectly to a series of events and circumstances. Such a view may even allow us to see an experience like religious conversion, which almost by definition is thought of as a one-time event, instead as a process unfolding over time.

The implications of understanding forgiveness as an emerging pathway through a changing landscape free us from the immediate pressure of a thoughtless appeal for release or from the insensitive moral prescription to reconcile without careful reflection when reflection may be what's needed most.

Such a view also acknowledges that each person or party is following a unique pathway, with its own history, timing, direction, and internal processes. Even though it may follow that of others, such a pathway progresses at its own pace, according to its own needs and ability to overcome the many possible obstacles. Its clarity of direction may only come from retracing steps again and again. Such an image challenges the notion that "going around and around" in circles means getting nowhere; a different perspective understands the circles (or re-cycling) of life as allowing us to go deeper into ever-maturing relationships and depths of understanding.[21]

Finally, forgiveness as pathway recognizes that my readiness to move beyond injury toward greater independence (or a healthier interdependence) and take a risk for reconciling is just that—my own readiness. Our experiences and level of emotional maturity uniquely prepare us for the journey, whether individually or collectively. A roadblock in the form of the rejection of my overture, offer, or request need not be seen only as a refusal to reconcile, a foregoing of forgiveness, a reason to turn back. Knowing that others too are walking along pathways of their own discoveries, undergoing a process that may yet lead to their own readiness, can be enough to keep us walking along the path in the hope of a healing encounter.

## BEYOND INJURY

Forgiveness is inextricably tied to injury. Apropos of our metaphor, a Chinese proverb suggests that "If you take one step in the wrong direction, a hundred steps in the right direction will not atone for it." Among the many other steps, injury invites the offender to reflection, apology, and restitution, if there is to be the possibility of forgiveness. To suggest another metaphor, beyond the initial harm and—if there has been one—apology, the ball is back in the court of the victim.

But just like a long tennis rally, no single volley is simply an isolated response to that which immediately precedes it. Opponents may have a long history of one-sided meetings. Prior matches with others may have exacted a greater toll on one player than another, the effects felt with each stroke. A lopsided or close score, the loss of a questionable call, the anticipation of victory, or the shifting support of the crowd may all influence any given point, perhaps all at once.

At any place in this interaction, the offended party may be asked, expected, invited, required, compelled—or simply choose—to respond to the offender's injurious action. The stories above only begin to illustrate the many types of responses that might follow. An apology may not be intended to elicit, and may not lead to, forgiveness. An apology may be outright refused and desired forgiveness withheld. Forgiveness may be cautiously made available in exchange for expected reparations. Or forgiveness may appear like an unexpected but needed gift of grace, offered on the way to reconciliation and healing. But what happens along the way?

## WITHDRAWAL AND REFLECTION

Hiking along one of my favorite Sierra trails has more than once led to a surprise encounter with a black bear. Though I always provide the distance worthy of these impressive animals, I don't ever recall having to stop and abandon my plans to reach my destination. However, there have been occasions when, after waiting long enough to determine that the bear has no intention of moving along, I have retreated to safely find another route to my desired goal. One particularly unpleasant encounter taught me to withdraw from the possibility of a confrontation, the outcome of which would have decidedly not been in my favor.

Withdrawal that is not necessarily overlooking, excusing, avoidance, or denial is a normal reaction to hurt. We may be immediately protecting our self from a reoccurrence of the offense, insuring as best we can against re-victimization (the justified "flight" in "fight or flight"). We may be grieving that which we had not imagined possible in a relationship or find ourselves lost in the pain of our loss.[22] Whether needed for a moment or a month, whether physical separation is required or only a degree of emotional distance, a healthy withdrawal can lead to additional reflection.

So what makes for a constructive withdrawal? Stepping back can provide an opportunity for reflection on the harm done to the relationship and one's reaction to it. It can be a good idea to limit one's rehearsal of events surrounding the injury, though the time needed for withdrawal might be short or long.

Contrary to the popular notion that lashing out at a substitute (pillows, walls, or other objects) dissipates the felt anger of a hurt, research has shown the opposite effect: The unconstructive rehearsing of anger is the practicing of destructive anger. The initial relief felt from the release of emotional energy only reinforces the notion that such behavior "works," at least in the moment, diverting one from the need to address underlying causes of hurt and anger. But its longer-term effect is all too often seen in the harm of future incidents.[23]

The process of reflection can involve other persons, including members of the community to which one belongs (whether victim or offender) to aid in discernment for this critical time. In the case of the Amish described earlier, the inseparability of individual from the community and its central values virtually eliminated the need to reflect on forgiveness as a choice to be made (or not).

Whether immediately or gradually reconciled, reflection can give us a chance to resolve the conflict between our "head" and our "heart"[24] in responding to injury, bringing together the direction set by what we (or others) think or believe ought to be with the reality of where we are emotionally. To shortcut or avoid this process altogether can create confusion or additional hurdles for moving forward. The consequences for forgiveness can be significant.

One summer I took a trip with my family and a group of friends to the central California coast. One friend was an avid surfer. Having previously tried this challenging sport, I was happy to stay back with the others on the beach to watch his efforts. Momentarily distracted, we heard a yell over the roar of the waves and turned to see him hobbling to the shore, barely able to make his way out of the surf. As he rode near the back of his board, a wave had thrust the nose of the board into the sandy bottom. His leg whipped around the bottom of the board, driving one of the sharp-edged scags (underwater fin) through his wetsuit and down into his thigh bone.

We rushed him to the emergency room and, after he had been taken care of, the doctor took my wife and me aside. He had cleaned the wound as much as possible, he said, but was leaving a tube in to help with draining. The worst-case scenario was that the external layer of skin would heal before the internal muscle tissue. If any debris or bacteria remained after its closing, the wound could become infected and would need to be opened up again. It wasn't until after his leg healed that we told our friend we had been informed of this unpleasant possibility kept from him at the time.

Similarly, any attempt to make a significant emotional hurt pass too quickly can cause complications later on if unresolved issues from past injuries surface unexpectedly to re-open a wound once thought healed. Like our friend, even more dangerous is the possibility that they don't surface at all, causing unseen damage. Such reflection can be painful and difficult. When explored in depth, we can begin to ask, Where has this come up before? What previous injury or trauma is the present one bringing to mind? The goal for such reflection is not to unnecessarily dig up past hurts but to become aware of the ways in which previous injuries continue to function in our emotional lives. The more we are aware of them, the less power they exert over us for determining our responses.

A final point of reflection relates to our sense of power (or powerlessness), especially as victims. Among other perspectives, a relational way of understanding power highlights the degree to which we are dependent upon other persons. It is not unusual in conflict for both parties to feel victimized to some degree, and, along with that feeling, have a sense of powerlessness.

But rarely are we ever completely without any power. Even in situations of seemingly great disparity, the interdependence that is minimally necessary to share a conflict, along with our sense of mutual reliance to either continue with or resolve the conflict, suggests that each party has some power in relation to the other. Rarely are we completely at the mercy of others in determining our response. We may not have much power, but it is likely that we have some. And our awareness of what that might be can help in the mutuality of the forgiveness process.

## Stuck Along the Path

As suggested above, reflection gives our heart the opportunity to catch up to our head, or it at least asks the part of us that serves as a compass for where we might go to wait until the injured self is ready to come along in that direction. Eventually we may decide to take another step. This point in our journey may be thought of as having come to a bridge, and we again ask ourselves if we are ready to make another decision for moving forward, crossing the gap that divides.

But sometimes we have taken the time to properly reflect, have prepared ourselves to continue the journey, and find that we are still stuck. "I'll simply never be able to forgive him." "I've tried everything, and I still can't find it within myself to forgive." "I even want to forgive—but can't." Here we may be confusing the journey with the destination. Having made one or more decisions at various points, we feel that forgiveness has already been granted. Having oriented our compass toward reconciliation (on our own or with the "encouragement" of someone else), we assume that we have accomplished the requisite task of forgiveness at the needed point along the way.

In guiding a congregation through a process of reconciliation after a long and painful experience of conflict, one person I'll call "Laura" confided to me her inability to forgive someone she saw as significantly responsible for the dispute. He had accepted responsibility for his actions and acknowledged how hurtful they had been, but she just couldn't find her way to forgiving him. "I don't know what's the matter," she said, "but I'm just not ready yet. Maybe I'll never be."

Having sensed others' willingness to reconcile, the pressure was great for all to move forward, but she couldn't pretend she was ready.

"So don't pretend," I suggested in a private conversation. I sensed she thought I was asking her to get past it, to "let go and let God" as someone else had tritely urged. "What I mean," I clarified, "is don't forgive if you're not ready."

She looked at me as if I were putting her through some kind of test. "But that's what we've been talking about this whole weekend . . . forgiving each other," she said, mostly checking to see if she had heard me right.

"You're right," I told her. "But you do want to forgive, and you'll be ready when you're ready. And if you're not ready just yet, that's okay. I'll talk to the group about the importance of letting everybody proceed at their own pace. We'll make sure there's permission for everyone to be right where they are. You're stuck right now. So just be stuck and see what happens."

"I guess I am," she acknowledged. "But you're sure that's okay?" she asked, checking one more time.

"Yes," I assured her. "Let's talk about it in the group after the break."

I knew it still wouldn't be easy for her to be seen as holding up the group's progress, so when she approached me just before we re-gathered, I expected her to say that she didn't want to hold back the group and would just say nothing. Either that or she was leaving all together.

"We talked," she told me in the hallway just outside the meeting room.

"You talked with the group already?"

"No, I talked to Ron," she said, naming the member with whom she was having so much difficulty.

"But I thought you were stuck," I said, trying not to sound too surprised.

"Yeah, I was. But your telling me it was okay helped me to admit I really was stuck and was not just being difficult. And once I realized that, I no longer felt stuck! I'm ready to at least start forgiving and join the group in moving forward."

Yet another paradox of forgiveness is that it may not be possible until we stop trying. When we're "stuck," that might mean that we should stop trying to get unstuck (or at least stop trying in a certain way).

My boys like to watch a popular survival show on TV. One regular piece of advice in life-threatening situations is to remain calm and resist the initial urge to simply try harder to get out. This is not easy, but it strikes me that working to get unstuck emotionally in trying to forgive is a lot like what needs to be done to get out of freezing water or quicksand. The more you struggle, at least in the way that seems natural, the less your chances of survival.

For both types of situations, being willing to stay in what can be an extremely uncomfortable environment long enough to find the proper means to get out seems counterintuitive at first but actually helps you find your way more clearly. The important thing about the path to forgiveness is not speed, but whether we can discover it at all.

We may also be stuck because our efforts are simply so focused on the point of blockage that we don't see (or even look for) another way around. Wilderness survival experts point out that when lost hikers are overwhelmed by a particular circumstance, their inability to move past it can begin a downward spiral of despair that leads to inactivity, even for meeting the most basic needs for food or shelter, sometimes producing tragic consequences.

In such a case, making constant—even if wrong—decisions about what is needed to survive is better than making no decision at all. Deciding to "give up" on a particular effort may lead one down another, even if unknown, path where a solution to the previous problem may be unexpectedly found.

Being stuck is another point at which being aware of power dynamics can be helpful. When we cannot see a way forward, we can feel helpless, powerless. Despite the pressure Laura felt from the group in the situation above, she held considerable power to prevent the group from moving forward. If I had suggested to her that she was wielding that power irresponsibly (I didn't think she was), she likely would have become defensive and even denied having the power, all the while continuing to use it.

But I also wanted not to call too much attention to Laura's power. Paradoxically, I did that by encouraging her to use it by (temporarily) withholding forgiveness. Urging those who are stuck to forgive may remind them of a good reason to stay stuck—it preserves the feeling of power they have and may see as the only means for getting remaining needs addressed, providing hope that justice might be done.

## EXTENDING GRACE

The difficult process of self-reflection that can accompany injury points to an important principle: offering forgiveness is something you do for yourself as well as for others.[25] Research supports the attitudes and practices associated with forgiveness as having a significant effect on our physical as well as emotional health, citing such benefits as the reduction of hostility and anger, improved cardiovascular functioning, the lowering of stress, and an increased ability to deal with and recover from illness. Some have gone so far as to not only tout the personal benefits of forgiveness but also to see almost any health problem as a sign of poor spiritual health resulting from unforgiveness.[26]

However positive such benefits may be, some might see such studies as taking too "instrumental" a view of forgiveness, designed primarily to underscore forgiveness as something one ought to do in the service of some other good. Perhaps there are some who forgive as a kind of rational calculation about its effect on the self.

Nevertheless, based on what we know about the complexities of internal human processes, extending forgiveness is not best thought of as the result of rational, cost-benefit analysis any more than is the act of injury which precedes it.

The experience of guilt, shame, and the construction of personal defenses can make offering forgiveness difficult. Unchecked forms or measures of each can limit our capacity to experience a key ingredient of forgiveness: empathy for the other. I remember some of my early experiences in victim-offender conferences. I was especially struck by how little often separated the careless acts of young offenders from what I recalled of my own actions as a youth. Neither their behavior nor mine is to be excused, but I was at least able to understand where such thoughtlessness and indifference came from. Just as that kind of insight and understanding can help offenders more fully to realize the effects of their behavior on victims, so too can it help victims to understand, empathize with and at times even develop a sense of compassion for their offenders.

In whatever ways they may emerge, empathy and compassion are about seeing the other as more like than different from me. However, that realization is not easy to come by as we may become convinced not only of the wrongness of the other's behavior but of the very evilness of their nature. Just as "blaming the victim" can be an unconscious way of trying to convince ourselves that we can prevent our own victimization, this tendency[27] provides the basis for justifying a lack of forgiveness of others.

Thus when we conclude that the utterly inhuman behavior of those who perpetrate atrocities can come only from "monsters" or "animals," this is a convenient way of reminding (convincing?) ourselves that we could never act in such a way. We need unforgivable persons to be something other than human partly because we want to believe that we could never commit such acts but even more deeply because we see our own need for forgiveness as human beings. The judgment required by forgiveness is turned upon ourselves. Patton best describes the paradox: "I am able to forgive when I discover that I am in no position to forgive."[28]

Though no guarantee, an apology can help with these critical intrapersonal and interactional aspects of forgiveness. This is partly because we get in touch with both our own story and that of the other in the exchange. As the saying goes, "An enemy is one whose story we have not heard." This applies not only to the other but to self since, as noted above, we can be our own worst enemy along the way.

As we'll see in the next chapter, apology provides for three key sets of "Rs"—recognition and responsibility, regret and remorse, and redress and reform—that highlight how power is actively at work in these internal and external processes of forgiveness. It is to that important dynamic of power that we now turn.

*Chapter 3*

# THE POWER OF FORGIVENESS

Despite her determined efforts to memorize key facial features that would identify her rapist, twenty-two-year old Jennifer Thompson wrongfully identified Ronald Cotton—once in photos, again in a live line-up, and a third time in court—as the man guilty of the brutal crime committed against her. Eleven years later, with the help of DNA evidence, the real rapist was identified and Ronald Cotton was released from jail.

Following her initial disbelief, Jennifer Thompson struggled to overcome the terrible guilt and "suffocating, debilitating shame" of a mistake that turned Cotton's life upside down. Thompson came to the conclusion that only a face-to-face meeting with Ronald Cotton would help her get past it. Eventually they met at a local church.

"I started to cry immediately," she said. "And I looked at him, and I said, 'Ron, if I spent every second of every minute of every hour for the rest of my life telling you how sorry I am, it wouldn't come close to how my heart feels. I'm so sorry.'"[29]

## THE POWER OF APOLOGY

"I'm sorry." "I apologize." Or, as a more recently popular form might offer, "My bad." Such words, and the regret and sorrow they represent, are often critical for the transformation of harm into healing and release. As significant as such statements are in our attempts to deal with even the worst kinds of wrongdoing, it is also likely that we hear some form of apology almost every day. In that sense, like forgiveness, apologies can be both simple and complex, meaningful or not.

What does it mean to offer an apology? What must an apology include? How can we know that an apology is genuine or sincere, or comes from the proper intentions and motivation? Are other gestures or statements needed? Or do such expressions potentially undermine the basic requirements? Are there acts for which no apology can (or should) be offered? And what of the obligation which follows?

The study of apology is not yet being done to an extent comparable to forgiveness, though it seems to be gaining momentum. That is possible, in part, because one can see frequent accounts of apologies (or something approximating an apology) by public figures of all kinds—national and international leaders, religious spokespersons, corporate officials, sports stars, and a host of other celebrities and individuals. There is almost no limit to how much can be written about apologies, for it seems that there is a ready example for nearly every point or aspect to be discussed.[30]

Within the larger context of forgiveness, an apology represents a potential transition from disengagement to engagement, from saving face and self-repair to relational repair, and from past to future. Reconciliation may still move forward without (or before) forgiveness, but forgiveness is very difficult without apology.

I don't want the obvious relationship between apologies and forgiveness to keep us from seeing them as separate though related phenomena, each with their own unique features and complex dynamics. After all, the offering of an apology, however sincere or well considered, doesn't in any way guarantee the granting of forgiveness any more than forgiveness makes reconciliation a certainty. In that sense, they are distinct.

However, the very context and cause for an apology provides for the possibility of forgiveness. They are both part of a dynamic interactive process between two parties united by the occurrence of injury. The interactive nature of apology is revealed by the language used; in English we say one "owes," "gives," "offers," "receives," or "accepts" an apology, implying exchange.

Furthermore, this language of interaction provided by apology emphasizes the importance to forgiveness of understanding what it means to be forgiven as much as what it means to forgive. As it turns out, the two are closely related, and recognizing the need to be forgiven applies to both offender and offended.

## THE STRUCTURE OF APOLOGIES

Similar to the overall approach being taken here for understanding forgiveness, I want to suggest, without diminishing the importance of any single element of an apology, that apologies might take different forms and have many different meanings.[31] As an interactive exchange, it is clear that an apology should be made by the identified offender and addressed to the victim whenever possible. The clear identification of offender and victim, and who owes whom what, can become the first point of contention and may indeed be an arguable distinction, but once an apology is offered it may also be the basis for further dialogue.

While in daily interactions we might occasionally hear a semblance of an apology offered in advance of an anticipated offense (for example, "I apologize for needing to leave early tonight"),[32] apologies can occur any time from immediately after a violation to years or even decades later. Both advantages and disadvantages can be found for a prompt or delayed response.

Much of what might be needed in response to a harm done may be implied in a simple "I'm sorry" or even a gesture. Many a time I have tried to convey my *mea culpa* to another driver on the road when nothing other than a facial expression or shoulder shrug was possible. With other kinds of gestures in mind, one can as easily indicate responsibility and remorse nonverbally as one can suggest blame and anger in such settings. Context will help determine how such messages are sent and received, both with respect to their intent and their adequacy in addressing the infraction.

Other things help to give meaning to apologies. Since apologies may consist of different aspects that take different shape from one setting, person, or relationship to the next, we might best think in terms of different forms or types of apologies as we have with other aspects of forgiveness. This suggests the possibility of a continuum of responses and a combination of elements, both verbal and nonverbal, by those who recognize that they have committed an offense. It also underscores the notion that conflict and its resolution are what sociologists and anthropologists call "socially constructed" activities in which people actively participate in the creation of meaning.[33]

## RECOGNITION AND RESPONSIBILITY

Not all wrongdoing or harm is recognized, and in such cases forgiveness may not be pursued through any means, at least as a mutual process. Given that possibility, for various reasons victims may need to find a way to initiate a process of healing from within. In such cases, victims seeking forgiveness and healing are not to be held hostage to the "moral awakening" of offenders.[34] However, when harm is recognized, an important place to start is with the behavior that provides the real or perceived need for an apology. Even before an acknowledgment of harm is offered, a request for an explanation of exactly what happened may help determine whether an apology is needed or called for. Once offered, an explanation itself can become a point of contention over an incident and conflict may revolve around discernment of intent, responsibility, and meaning.

It is possible that the acknowledgment of wrongdoing will be accompanied by a "call" for an apology. This call may come from an offender's internal response to feelings of guilt or shame based on values shared with family, wider community, or victim. Beyond the offender's conscience, the victim or others offended by an act of wrongdoing may call for the acknowledgment of harm done that an apology provides. To the victim, this is the initial sign that the perpetrator accepts responsibility for what was done, and it provides recognition and validation of suffering caused.[35]

But explanations can also serve as the means for denying full (or any) responsibility for harm done. Perhaps having already justified one's behavior to oneself, the offering of an explanation or an account of one's actions may be the most likely alternative response to the call for an apology that acknowledges wrongdoing. Such an explanation may come from the creation of a self-preserving mental scenario intended to provide "the least incriminating, most plausible account of the situation, congruent with one's pride structure"[36] and offered as a reasonable, justifiable rationale for one's behavior, however regrettable. "Had you been in my shoes," it suggests, "you would have done the same thing."

Though perhaps mistaken for or even intended as an apology, providing an account may be an unconscious attempt to excuse one's self from responsibility or consequences. Such an explanation is, after all, proffered as a reasonable defense of one's behavior, a distancing of self from blameworthy actions. An appeal to reason inevitably points outward, beyond ourselves to external factors and forces beyond our control. Genuine apologies are difficult in part because they point inward, where rational appeals to an impaired self or diminished capacity come across as poor excuses. ("That was not like me to do that," or "I don't know what came over me."). We might say, then, that the first effect of an apology is on the self.

In some cultures apology does not allow for the questioning of responsibility. The very language of apology may contain direct references to or acceptance of blame, guilt, or culpability. Presumably, even if one doubts one's responsibility for wrongdoing, no rationalizing, justifying, or qualifying account of one's behavior is possible once the apology is offered. However, if such doubts exist an apology may not be forthcoming.

On the other end of the continuum where acceptance by and attachment to the injured party are the motivators, the (alleged) offender may comply with all requests, demands, or conditions in appeasement of the victim. The possibility here is that, in the attempt to maintain relationship and regain intimacy through conciliation, the offender may seek to placate the victim at almost any cost to self, without risking discernment of responsibility or the working through of legitimate differences, perhaps without ever dealing with the hurt and breach of the relationship.

If the extremes of separation or attachment are avoided through a more healthy attempt to work through the issues of an offense, however painfully, an apology may include or be accompanied by a recollection of the offense. In his widely recognized sociological work on apology, Nicholas Tavuchis suggests that an apology must first name the facts of the offense.[37] Here a second type of "call" takes place for the offender: the recall of one's harmful actions. This is no small thing and has different significance for each party, as an Angolan proverb suggests: "The one who throws the stone forgets; the one who is hit remembers forever."[38] An apology retells or recounts the facts of the offense in a way that recalls the harm done. It's simply, "I did this" without an explanation of why.

In many cases it is important that the specific harm be identified. Once when consulting with a church in conflict, a man stood to address the group: "If I ever offended anyone here in any way," he offered, "I ask that you forgive me." Later, persons who clearly recalled having been hit by very specific "stones" of this would-be confessor withheld any assurance of forgiveness, unsure if he was even aware of the harm done. In the same way, one too often hears leaders accept "full responsibility" for actions without seemingly realizing any consequences for doing so, as if the words performed some magical "righting" function on their own.

## Regret and remorse

As a basic form of speech some have argued that, beyond the acknowledgment and acceptance of responsibility for a specific harm, the only other requirement of a (spoken) apology is the expression of sorrow and regret (or remorse), following which nothing more is to be done other than await the response of the injured party. While acknowledging responsibility as a matter of factual record can seem straightforward, an expression of regret can mean, refer to, or rely on many things, some of which may threaten to undermine the acceptance of blame or outright indicate no intention or realized need to apologize.

That's partly because the words of sorrow and regret can convey other emotions, such as sadness, or be directed toward things other than blameworthy behavior. For example, a parent commenting on a disciplinary measure might say to a grounded teenager, "I'm sorry that this means you will be missing out on your activity this weekend," while still being convinced of the appropriateness of the discipline. It is even likely that the parent will have in mind the teen's behavior as the cause of such consequences.

One can certainly express the wish that things could have been otherwise without admitting that one has done anything wrong. A common expression of regret that often seeks to pass as an apology similarly blames the victim for the outcome or their regrettable response to it. A statement such as, "I'm sorry you took such offense at my comment" implies that it is your sensitivity, rather than my indiscretion, that is the problem.

Other possibilities further cloud the significance of sorrow and regret. I can regret the acts of persons other than myself; I can regret the effect of my behavior on others rather than the intended objective even if realized (as in the case of parental discipline above); I can regret having been caught in the act of wrongdoing without regretting the effect that it had on others; likewise, I might primarily or only regret the consequences about to be realized for my self for behavior injurious to others ("If I had only been more careful about being caught").

In such cases, an "apology" may be intended to help one's self get off the hook without admitting responsibility. A *New Yorker* cartoon illustrates the delicateness of this dance. At the counter of a florist shop, a man asks the clerk,

"What flower says you're sorry without admitting wrongdoing?"[39]

A more complicated dilemma can exist even when a spoken apology seems to recognize the harm done, accept responsibility, and give evidence of sorrow and remorse. The child on the receiving end of a parent-directed apology ("You tell her you're sorry right now!") immediately suspects that the expression of regret is merely following expectations or the demand and is not heartfelt or genuine. (On more than one occasion I have heard the quick sibling retort to such an apology: "No you're not!") Even heartfelt regret can be doubted when its impetus for being expressed is perceived to be externally rather than internally generated; that is, the regrest is the result of coercion or merely remorse over consequences rather than recognition of moral failure.

A compelled apology does not guarantee the recognition of moral failure. We might say that the spoken word needs additional support from other emotions, gestures, and signs to give it the meaning the victim may be looking for.

## REDRESS AND REFORM

If an apology or a request for forgiveness is believed to be false or for some other reason violates our sense of justice, it can provoke outrage or even violence in response.[40] We may need, expect, demand or otherwise look for signs of certain attitudes, emotions, motivations, and intentions—such as honesty, sincerity, empathy, humility, and remorse—that we otherwise have no means to confirm as genuine. We cannot know the hearts of persons. For some, no action beyond a verbal apology may be needed, especially if reconciliation is not pursued or desired at the time. For others, a single encounter with deception can turn the most trusting person into a skeptic. But where relationships continue in some form, a victim's need for restitution and assurance of future safety may be of utmost importance.

The various meanings related to future action suggest that the promises of apologies also require clarification, though absolute certainty of an offender's commitment is not possible to achieve. This may mean that an appropriately qualified commitment to change will give an apology more integrity than unconditional guarantees: "I will do everything possible to make sure I never do that again"; "I commit myself to make every effort to resist that behavior"; "I want you to know that I have every intent to not repeat my actions," etc.

A commitment that speaks to one's intent to reform is perhaps the best that can be provided by a statement alone. Unfortunately, a victim's need for certainty about change in the offender and an offender's desire to meet that need may not only permit guarantees with little basis to go untested— but may also encourage such unqualified assurances and their unquestioned acceptance to proceed without recognition of their limitations.

In some cases it is to be expected that genuine remorse which recognizes that harmful behavior is a moral failure will immediately be followed up with evidence that the behavior will not be repeated. This is particularly important for certain types of harm since expressions of remorse are known to be part of abuse cycles. Where trust does not exist, it may be that only time can provide the assurance a victim needs that harmful behavior will not be repeated. While it is not possible to guarantee such a promise, each successful avoidance of undesirable behavior—especially when similar conditions or opportunities present themselves—can serve as a rung on the ladder of trust.

Those who believe in the possibility of change do the best they can by relying on other, more outwardly identifiable signs to help them, such as that which comes from reparation and living up to commitments. In 1998, Katherine Power became eligible for parole after serving five years in prison for her role in a bank robbery that resulted in the death of police officer Walter Schroeder. What's unusual about the case is that Power was convicted after avoiding authorities for twenty-three years as one of the FBI's ten most wanted criminals in association with the activities of a militant anti-Vietnam war group, including Officer Schroeder's death. After turning herself in out of concern for her own family's life, Power began her eight-to-twelve year sentence with little remorse for her involvement and its effect on Schroeder's family.

But after five years of work "peeling back the layers of defensiveness," Katherine came to accept full responsibility for her actions and apologized to members of the Schroeder family. They were finally satisfied with what they heard at her parole hearing but noted that, because it was in Power's self-interest to say the right words, doubts would remain. That was not enough for Power, who took the unheard-of step of withdrawing her request for parole as a sign that she would not be content as long as her statement was attached to the possibility of leaving prison. She agreed to stay beyond what might have been required as an expression of remorse.[41]

From this we can understand how attempts at redress may be thought of as disingenuous or seeking to undo that from the past which cannot be undone. At the least, forms of restitution represent the attempt to make right that which has been recognized as wrong, less as an actual undoing of the past and more as a sign of genuine repentance and intention for the future.

But even if a spoken apology and any related actions by an offender help offender and victim move toward shared goals (such as forgiveness), each response can still have different meaning for each party. That may place the parties' goals at risk. For example, an offer of monetary reparation may for one person serve as an adequate symbolic representation of appropriate remorse and a sign of expected reform, yet a different victim may take the same offering as a completely inadequate reparation for that which has been lost. This has been true, for example, in cases of sexual abuse by clergy.

On the other hand, since motives and intent cannot be known with certainty, a disguised, self-serving apology may have just as much of a chance at initiating a transformative process of healing for one or both parties, though we might hope and look for better. In such instances, an offender, doubting or not caring about the significance of an apology for a victim may be unexpectedly moved by a victim's acceptance and gracious offer of release, sparking a response of genuine remorse upon which reform can be built.

## NEGOTIATIONS

The interactions described above have given rise to some debate about the appropriateness of negotiating over apologies, or any part of forgiveness. Negotiations about statements or actions may be thought of primarily as clarifications or corrections to misunderstood or inadequate first attempts at apology. Formal negotiations about apologies are more likely to occur in the national or international arena where public statements are closely scrutinized for considerations of both parties' interests, and the need to save face is crucial for ongoing relationships in which acknowledging responsibility for past harms may have significant implications for reparations.

Any aspects of a stated apology considered essential might also be thought of as non-negotiable. Those elements more in need of mutual clarification—from who should apologize (say, when a group is involved) to what exactly should be acknowledged, offered, expected, or accepted— are more likely to be understood as negotiable. But because each aspect of an apology can have different significance for different persons, we may not be able to determine what elements are negotiable outside of a specific context. Even if certain aspects (e.g., reparations) were considered necessary for a full and meaningful apology, their content might need to be mutually determined.

However, like forgiveness, some equate any "negotiation" of apology with any commodification in which required compensation serves to override the moral obligation to redress wrongful behavior. As noted above, there exists concern that required expressions of promised changes may inadvertently suggest the possibility of the earned reversibility of harm done.

Kraybill suggests that "negotiations should never be viewed as punishment or retribution, notions which may trivialize the gravity of the damage by suggesting that inflicting hurt on an aggressor is somehow adequate compensation to those who suffered."[42] An aspect of this concern is how any required response from the offender, as part of interactive exchange with the victim, is followed by the expectation of and corresponding call for reciprocity from the victim in the form of sympathy and release. From this emerges the need to examine the dynamic of power in apology.

## THE DYNAMICS OF POWER

Though potentially transformational, we may not be able to fully escape the less benign, constantly shifting power dynamics in the course of interactions in which the need for apology emerges. When confronted with the human inclination to use power in destructive ways, it is important to understand what role it plays in forgiveness and, in particular, apology.

Another favorite *New Yorker* cartoon[43] shows a man groveling on the floor in contrition, holding forth a large bouquet of flowers to a woman seated in a chair. Barely bothering to acknowledge his presence, the woman turns from her morning paper and coffee and says, "Don't you *dare* apologize to me!" Still another shows two men dressed in clerical garb standing alongside their just-wrecked vehicles. There they vie for the moral high ground. "Now hold it right there!" says one to the other. "If there's going to be any forgiving done it will be done by me!"

Humorous yet pointed, these cartoons provide insight into the subtle but often missed issues that deserve our attention as we consider the role that apology has in forgiveness, reconciliation, and healing. The first cartoon suggests that, no matter how important, an apology may not suffice to make amends . . . or even be wanted. As difficult as a genuine apology can be to offer, one faces the very real possibility that the person harmed may not be ready or willing to receive or accept it. As a potential form of manipulation, aggrieved persons may even see apologies as one more thing against which they must protect themselves.

On the other hand, a desire to apologize may trigger a shift in the balance of power so that the one harmed gains the upper hand over the once-powerful offender. But even then the pressure is great: Once an apology has been offered, any reluctance to accept the apology and offer forgiveness can be seen as ungraciousness or a form of vengeful punishment enacted by withholding an expected response to a recognized good.

This acknowledgment of shifting power is also reflected in the cartoon involving the two clerics. One can imagine the retort, "Now hold it right there!" following quickly on the heels of the other's unsolicited pronouncement of forgiveness. The unstated but clearly implied offer is less a merciful response to sincere contrition than a preemptive attempt to assume moral superiority by assigning fault for injury. Both cartoons imply something seldom acknowledged: that, when accompanied by a contrite offender who recognizes wrongdoing and desires forgiveness, being the victim can provide one with a measure of power and control all the more tempting to wield on the heels of an injury suffered.

Apology and pardoning of the other are only two parts of the forgiveness equation. A third cartoon highlights yet another. A woman, sitting on a couch with arms crossed and body turned away from a man on a nearby chair, looks his way and says matter-of-factly, "Of course I can forgive you, but how can you forgive yourself?" This is no simple query, but a weapon that at once says "I am big enough to forgive even that, but no one who would do such a thing could possibly live with—let alone forgive—his or her self."

At times, forgiveness between can be blocked by the absence of forgiveness within. We may not recognize the need to forgive ourselves for our perceived or real part in wrongdoing, related or not to the specific harm done to us. Or, as our third cartoon suggests, though recognized, forgiving ourselves may be the most difficult task of all. Our offensive behavior, amplified by the undeserving offer of grace by another, may bring to mind the shortcomings we see inside that go deeper than a single incident. Our concern for what we have done deepens to a concern for who we have become.

The guilt and shame of moral failure makes apologizing to another difficult and may include more demanding introspection. Offenders face not only the harm caused and negative effects on their standing in a larger community—but also painful self-reflection about character and identity which may be significantly at odds with prior self-image.

At the deepest level, in relation to the particular wrongdoing, offenders may fear being judged "unforgivable." This may be a powerful negative motivator never to apologize or seek forgiveness, especially when offenders feel thsmelves undeserving, a suspicion better left unconfirmed.

Finally, it may seem to offenders that apologies needed or desired by the victims are the last elements within offenders' control in the process of forgiveness or reconciliation (or merely ongoing relationship). Offenders may experience withholding of an expected apology as the last power over the victim. Holding onto this power becomes a strong temptation regardless of (or perhaps because of) how badly offenders may feel. Whatever burdens are hence placed on the victim to respond, after an apology is made offenders will be entirely at the victim's mercy.

As one author puts it, forgiveness is a "profound transaction."[44] Once given, an apology "cannot go unnoticed without [further] compromising the current and future relationship of the parties, the legitimacy of the violated rule, and the wider social web in which the participants are enmeshed."[45] The victim's response in the cartoon mentioned above ("Don't you dare apologize!") calls our attention to the shifting sense of obligation from offender to victim that an apology might signal.

One not unimportant expectation is that the offended party graciously accept the apology, though one should be prepared for the possibility of rejection. A popular comic illustrates this well.[46] As father and son sit at the kitchen table enjoying ice cream being served by the man's wife, she takes the opportunity to apologize. "I'm sorry I've been so grouchy today," she offers. His response is clearly not what was expected: "How about yesterday?" he asks. In the final frame, the son comments to the man, ice cream sundae sitting squarely on his head complete with a cherry on top: "I'm glad you don't work for the State Department."

Once offered an apology, the victim is asked to believe, to understand, to accept, to now assume the moral obligation for converting feelings of betrayal, anger, and indignation into forgiveness. For some, this is simply too much to ask. The moral obligation an apology can impose does underscore the importance of a stated apology in a conflict's transition toward forgiveness. However, it perhaps overemphasizes apology as a one-time statement absent consideration of the other components discussed throughout this chapter.

The power dynamic identified in the victim-offender transaction may fail to convey the broader meaning of apology as ongoing beyond initial words of acknowledgment and sorrow or regret. In other words, a shift in obligation and a change in power takes place only to the degree that an apology is perceived as being complete in itself—with nothing else required of the offender.

Once apologized to, however, the victim may only be able to hold onto the forgiveness card for so long before it loses its place in a meaningful exchange. As one victim put it, "If we wait for an offender to apologize in the way I require, it may never come."[47]

Conversely, the more we think of forgiveness as something done, something granted in a generous one-time act following an apology, the more we can appreciate an apology as an act of power preceding a "final pronouncement."

The power that potentially comes with the victim's moral obligation to release the offender is not only derived from the fulfilled obligation of the offender's apology. This is a complex dynamic. Power is potentially gained and lost in the same interaction. A victim's need for an apology (which gives power to the offender) occurs in the context of both parties' anticipation that the offered apology will represent a shift in power back to the victim. As long as forgiveness is withheld or even pending, the injurer still owes (or is perceived to owe) the injured something.

Victims' unwillingness or inability to forgive may be the self-protective use of the only power they perceive themselves to have. People who say, "I can't" (forgive), may be saying that they feel powerless to give up their power![48]

However, shifting yet again, the greater the expectation that an apology compels forgiveness, the more the onus for action reverts back to the victim, threatening to undo whatever efforts have been made to empower the victim to overcome the harms of the past. A victim may express forgiveness in response to the felt expectation that it is the noble thing to do.

But, even if freely offering forgiveness in response to an offender's apology, victims may yet find further opportunities to wield the lessened but not completely surrendered power of the forgiver. Victims may hold even this gift of grace at the ready as a guilt-inducing weapon: "You do remember how I forgave you for what you did!"

## BEYOND APOLOGY

The frequency of human injury creates countless opportunities for apology. Each presents a case study for analysis of the many elements explored in this chapter, line by line, word by word. That can be a helpful academic exercise, but instead of repeating here what others have done adequately elsewhere, I want to close this discussion of apology by anticipating where we will go next—to the response of forgiveness. A return to our opening story provides a moving example.

Jennifer Thompson had identified Ronald Cotton as the man who raped her, only to learn eleven years later that she had made a tragic mistake. After discovering the truth through DNA evidence that she had mistakenly helped put an innocent man in prison, they met and Jennifer apologized. "I asked Ron if he could ever forgive me. And with all the mercy in the world he took my hands and with tears in his eyes, he told me he had forgiven me a long time ago."

To her, Ronald Cotton had been a monster, and every day for those eleven years she had prayed that he would die . . . that he would be raped in prison and someone would kill him. "And here was this man," said Thompson, "who with grace and mercy just forgave me. How wrong I was, and how good he is."

Ronald and Jennifer consider themselves friends now, collaborating on projects to share their story of forgiveness. "Some people don't really understand it," says Ronald. "But we were the victims of the same injustice by the same man, and this gave us a common ground to stand on. Together we were able to help each other heal through a shared experience."

The power of forgiveness extends beyond the many transactions of apology in the larger process. That power extends both into the past and into the future, bringing both into the transforming present. Whether the gap between the past and the future can be bridged has significantly to do with whether one's sense of justice—whether full of demands or filled with grace—has been met. To that topic, and the significant role of memory in the process, we turn next.

*Chapter 4*

# THE JUSTICE OF FORGIVENESS

Far from perfect, the Truth and Reconciliation Commission set up in post-apartheid South Africa was criticized for providing amnesty to perpetrators and its failure to achieve real reconciliation between blacks and whites. As an important element in its transition to democracy, South Africa faced a choice between providing as many victims as possible with the opportunity to learn the truth about the fate of colleagues, friends, and loved ones, or pursuing full justice for relatively few. Like reconciliation processes conducted elsewhere, the process in many ways asked more of victims and survivors—to absorb, to risk, to accept, to tolerate, to manage, to offer grace and forgiveness—than it did of perpetrators.

One cannot yet fully know the long-term impact of the Commission's findings on individuals and, more importantly, South African society as a whole. However, South Africa chose to move into its unknown future with a bias toward reconciliation that rejects revenge and invites the possibility of forgiveness.[49]

Misguided reflection, or none at all, can lead to thoughts of revenge. Even as persons who disapprove of such responses, we can understand its origins. Vengeance reflects the heart's desire for justice. Justice, we might say, is vengeance that has learned its manners.[50] Demands for atonement, acknowledgment, punishment, penance, penitence, repentance, reparations, confession, contrition, consequences, remorse, regret, and recognition all express the need for justice. For many, these are necessary conditions to enable forgiveness even to be considered. For others, forgiveness comes as final recognition that a sufficient price has been paid. At the very least, forgiveness "might be thought of as the alternative to retaliation in settling a moral score."[51]

Beyond this, justice doesn't preclude mercy; it makes it possible.[52] However understood, justice rightly condemns harmful behavior and seeks to make right the offense. Offered conditionally, forgiveness may require some satisfaction of one's sense of justice, a balancing of ledgers from the past into the present through penitent action by the offender. Justice has many forms,[53] and those that lead to the acceptance of responsibility and provide for ongoing accountability are best.

It is easy to allow past hurts and injustices to accumulate unaddressed. The Amish work hard at keeping those ledgers balanced, both within the community and between their community and others; perhaps that is why they can forgive even the greatest offense so quickly and without need for reparation. For the rest of us, it can be a more arduous task.

Any honest assessment of the retributive U.S. justice system recognizes that it is severely broken and in need of repair. Even the harshest punishment can leave victims without a sense of satisfaction. This brings some to realize that those offenses that cannot be dealt with through punishment or restitution are not any more likely to be undone by our own "vigilance of anger and revenge."[54]

This also helps victims understand that the most critical needs they have can be met—perhaps only met—without hanging onto bitterness, resentment, hate, rage, and a desire for vengeance. For some, anger and rage not prematurely suppressed and rightly directed can prevent a further sense of self violation and powerlessness. However, for others, the more tightly held, the more these things can poison and eventually destroy the already injured party.

Never best understood as a single decision, this too is one of the many possible choices of forgiveness: the decision to absorb the injury; to set aside one's claim on justice; to forego revenge; to dispense with the demand for retribution; to abandon the right to resentment; to interrupt the cycle of violence; to respond to, and overcome, evil with good; perhaps even to love one's enemy.

## CONDITIONAL AND UNCONDITIONAL

Whether forgiveness is demanding or freely offered, requires much, little, or nothing at all, raises the question of conditional and unconditional forgiveness. This problem gets at the heart of the place of justice in forgiveness.

For some, forgiveness is only possible under the right set of circumstances once all requirements have been met. This often includes the proper identification of the victim and readiness on his or her part, the recognition of harm done, a public acknowledgment (or confession) of complicity and guilt, and expression of true remorse, followed by a commitment to and demonstration of reformed behavior as evidence of the offender's sincere repentance. In this view, forgiveness is something that must be earned by the offender, even if what is lost can never be repaid and if only to lessen the burden on the one already bearing the injury. These things combine to help the forgiver become ready and the forgiven be recognized as worthy of working toward true forgiveness. Here forgiveness is conditional.

Despite how these high standards protect against "cheap grace," for some there are instances in which forgiveness is simply not possible no matter the effort. Because of the widely held principle, for example, that only victims may forgive, many consider the irrevocable and irreversible crime of murder to be unforgivable. For another to absolve a perpetrator of such crimes, it is thought, is to betray the memory of the victim and violate the sanctity of forgiveness. Ultimate examples of this include the Holocaust and other acts of genocide. In the end, some stains cannot be cleansed, neither by God, as some would argue, nor by persons.

But there is another view.

If the mystery of forgiveness, clarified but not defined or limited by the understandings above, is yet a miracle that can neither be fully explained nor intentionally manufactured, then true forgiveness consists of nothing more or less than in forgiving the unforgivable. Premised on the understanding that forgiveness is an unqualified gift of grace, there can therefore be no amount of earning, no exchange, no transaction or any other condition under which it can be offered. In cases of murder, some hold, this truly honors the dead, recognizing the ultimate expression of humanity's recognition of humanity. All forgiveness is unconditional.[55]

There are two perspectives on this second understanding. First, all preconditions for offering and receiving forgiveness are seen as reducing it to a kind of economic transaction. The more a request for forgiveness "makes sense" based on what an offender has said or done to account for his or her behavior, the less that person is in need of forgiveness. After all, the more wrongdoing can be explained so that its basis is understood, the more "reasonable" such behavior seems. The more reasonable the behavior, the more earned or justified any response of mercy or grace becomes; a logical exchange. "Under those circumstances," one might say, "I can see why you might have done that." But if earned or deserved, forgiveness is not a gift. By definition, a true gift can only be unconditional. "What would be a forgiveness that forgave only the forgivable?" Derrida asks.[56]

A second perspective on the unconditional nature of forgiveness is willingness to assume no "reasonableness" for offensive behavior. As a guilty and confessed offender who offers neither excuse nor explanation of bad behavior moves along the path of contrition and repentance, the newly transformed person is no longer the same as the one found culpable of the offense. Forgiveness can no more be granted to such a person than the same river can be stepped into twice, as the saying goes. To forgive the one who has met certain conditions (to change) is to forgive someone other than the one who is (was) guilty. Again, in this view, pure forgiveness can only be offered free of all conditions. Hence, the paradox of unconditional forgiveness: only the unforgivable can be forgiven.

To not have one's sense of justice satisfied and yet forgive is to forgive unconditionally. To forgive an offense for which justice is partly met is to release that which remains. But this is not merely the overlooking or disregarding of a small injury or slight. In such minor cases we neither condemn nor keep a ledger of debt owed. Even the full satisfaction of justice does not preclude the need for forgiveness. Such conditions may more readily lead to forgiveness and show how justice and forgiveness work hand-in-hand. Critical to these understandings is the central place of memory in the process of forgiveness.

## JUSTICE AND MEMORY

Justice has to do with redressing wrongs of the past. Within this process there is a significant role for memory. There is remembering involved in the recounting of one's pain and the effect of that pain on one's life. There is remembering involved in the naming and acknowledgment of wrongdoing that precedes or comes with apology. There is remembering involved in accepting responsibility for wrongdoing, seeking to make things right. There is remembering involved in standing alongside victims and their pain (including the pain of their memory). There is remembering involved in protecting one's self and others from future harm. And there is, in another sense, the re-membering of that which an injury has torn apart—the putting-back-together into one whole, whether for an interpersonal relationship or an entire country.

But what place does memory have once forgiveness has been offered and received? And how is memory related to that old adage, forgive and forget? I don't argue here for the importance of one (remembering or forgetting) over the other; rather, I want to examine what role each plays in the processes of forgiveness as another way for helping us understand what makes forgiveness confusing and difficult as well as meaningful and possible.

## FORGIVE AND FORGET?

As I get older, I find myself becoming increasingly forgetful—a normal, though perhaps troublesome, trend for a professor. I have never been one for being able to recall the small details of past events and experiences. When reminiscing with friends or family, I'm grateful for others' recollection of things I somehow have forgotten. But this has served me well in some ways too. While it can still take me some time to initially get over hurts and disappointments (ask my wife!), I have never had a very long memory even for more painful wrongs.

This too has its price. If my forgetting which serves as a kind of letting go of grudges is nothing more than "memory fatigue," then those injustices may not be any more forgotten than the experiences others are able to bring back to life for me in their recollection of past events. When we are recounting a shared happy experience, their memory of details I've forgotten often allows me to relive joys of the past. Just because I've forgotten the details doesn't mean that—with a little help—the feelings can't be conjured up, good and bad.

If I'm honest with myself, this can also be true for forgotten hurts not forgiven. In fact, I may have allowed myself to think that a past hurt was forgiven because it was forgotten. If I'm trying to recall something about a hurtful act from the past and ask someone else to help me with the details, I can find myself feeling angry or hurt or resentful all over again for the re-remembered act. However, the fact that I can also recall past injustices genuinely forgiven without the re-emergence of such feelings suggests that forgiving doesn't require forgetting but perhaps a different kind of remembering.

## REMEMBER

No one has advocated more strongly for the significance of memory than Elie Wiesel—Holocaust survivor, Nobel Peace Laureate, and author of more than fifty books. For Wiesel, remembering is about the past and the future, linking them to one another and each to the present; honoring the humanity and personhood of those who went before, being in their presence, saying "No" to forgetting acts of indignity, injustice, and death. To remember is to say "Yes," to create the possibility of justice, dignity, survival, the future. To remember is to be. In a word, says Wiesel, memory can be redemptive, the source of our salvation.[57]

Serbian journalist Zeljiko Vukovic highlights the more dangerous, shadow side of memory. He records the story of a Bosnian Muslim woman who, having taught her community's Serbian children to love through literature, was later subjected to their humiliating and painful acts of hate during the war because of her different ethno-religious identity. Her memories of their brutal treatment, and wish for revenge, led her to name her son Jihad, or holy war. She explained, "The first time I put my baby at my breast I told him, 'May this milk choke you if you forget.' So be it."[58]

The religious and secular injunction, Remember! (or, as stated in the negative, Never forget!) has not interrupted the ever-escalating spiral of human violence. Forgiveness requires an accounting of the past, and we human beings seem to have a special capacity for remembering the pain of wrongdoing done to us. But even if we reject the impulse toward vengeance as directed by a mother's memories, we must still come to terms with memories that can persist even beyond the offering and receiving of forgiveness.

In his insightful exploration of memory based partly on his own interrogation experience in Tito's Yugoslavia, Croatian born theologian Miroslav Volf wrestles with the question of remembering the wrongs of a violent world. Volf argues first that memory is important for acknowledging wrongdoing and for both identifying the offender and recognizing the victim. We must remember. But since remembering can lead to its own response of wrongdoing, Volf suggests that the central question is not whether we should remember but how to remember rightly.[59] A difficult but critical step in remembering rightly, particularly with regard to injustices, is to remember truthfully.

Forgiveness provides for complex understandings of and ways for engaging justice, truth, and memory. The fulfillment of Justice's demand relies on Truth's ability to expose wrongdoing, shining its light of honesty and transparency on behavior that causes injury and harm. But truth is often difficult to come by, not only because it can be experienced in many different ways but also because our memory can be selective, and all sides in a conflict may believe only they genuinely possess the truth. Such a belief is dangerous and often used to justify wrongdoing. In these ways, truth can be a hurdle to forgiveness, both because of the difficulty of that which may be required to make things right once discovered, and perhaps first of all because of our need to be right.[60]

Even more problematic is the fact that our processes of "justice" rarely reward the truth. Thus we unwittingly prevent the possibility of forgiveness and genuine reconciliation. An anecdote illustrates my point.

My family and I lived and worked among Aboriginal peoples in Labrador, Canada, with the Mennonite Central Committee for two years. During that time, I worked closely with community leaders committed to bringing healing to their people. On his way to town one day from his village, a respected Innu alcohol counselor came upon several men hitch-hiking along the side of the road. He invited the men into his truck and struck up a conversation about their destination.

All of the men were going to court, he discovered, for the same reason: disruptive behavior stemming from excessive drinking. "So what are you doing today?" he asked them. "Pleading not guilty," they each informed him without exception. "Oh, so you didn't do it?" he asked suspiciously but not accusingly. "Oh we did it," they freely told him, "but our lawyer says we need to plead not guilty." By the time they arrived at the court, this community leader had convinced all of them to tell the truth before the judge and accept responsibility for their behavior, stressing that it was the Innu way and the first step along the path to healing.

Later when I was working with the leaders of that same community to establish self-government community justice policies, they proposed an alternative to the normal RCMP (Royal Canadian Mounted Police) approach for interviewing crime victims and other witnesses. The usual procedures, they argued, conducted by outsiders, seldom resulted in the discovery of the truth. Concern for relationships and community was pushed aside out of concern for other things such as the determination of guilt or innocence. The Innu knew that community members, even offenders, would be more honest if they could first talk to other Innu they knew and trusted. This echoes Volf's concern that remembering is compelled to truthfulness by its obligation to do justice.[61]

## BEYOND MEMORY

Forgiveness is difficult not only because the truth can be illusive but also because we are not sure about its proper place in our memory. Just as hate can be the guardian against the loss of important memories,[62] memory of painful injuries can be the guardian of a remembered vulnerable self, protecting us from their reoccurrence. Rightly integrated into the whole of our life story, even the most painful memory can be understood as a meaningful part of our identities.[63] Its meaning can be determined only by ourselves and no one else, though we may connect it to others' stories of survival, solidarity, hope, liberation, love, redemption, or salvation.

But if our memories can be self-servingly selective, or susceptible to other problems of inaccuracy or being incomplete, would we be better off allowing ourselves to forget injuries of the past before we use them to bring about further harm? Modern research and technology is making this possible and perhaps ever more likely. The same efforts being conducted in neuroscience to improve or recover memory for Alzheimer's patients have also led to so-called "amnesia drugs" and other forms of treatment to edit, "dampen," or even erase memories of severe trauma or pain.

The possibility of using technology to "heal" us of such undesirable memories, and its unintended consequences, enters into popular culture through such movies as *Eternal Sunshine of the Spotless Mind*. Using a literary metaphor, the risks of such erasure have led some to suggest that a more desirable approach is the striking out of memories rather than their deletion. ~~For example, if I format a sentence in this way you must engage it somehow differently, even if you ignore it, than if I had excluded it from the text altogether~~. Still unsatisfied with these possibilities, we search for other metaphors or other ways of understanding old ones.

Despite all the important remembering required in the processes of forgiveness, Volf suggests that forgetting is the final step in moving toward a more redemptive outcome in the service of grace and reconciliation. Remembering that we need to be forgiven can help us to forgive others. He reminds us of Karl Barth's concern that we might not even be able to carry on with our lives if we didn't literally forget at least some—and probably most—of the wrongs we had ever committed. To forget that long list is a gift of grace that we freely offer to, and gladly receive from, ourselves. To treat others then, in this regard, as we would want ourselves to be treated is to at least acknowledge some type of forgetting as worthy of consideration.

But how might this work? Perhaps we can compare it to the difficulty and power of letting go of unjustified feelings of guilt. A scene from the movie *Good Will Hunting* illustrates this dynamic well. In a final meeting with his therapist, Matt Damon's title character is assured that he is not to blame for the severe physical abuse he endured at the hands of his foster father. The therapist, played by Robin Williams, simply states, "It's not your fault." Will responds casually at first, "Yeah, I know." This exchange is repeated three more times, and Will increasingly loses his patience with what he sees as the therapist's "game."

The therapist, sensing that the significance of the statement is not fully sinking in, presses his point four more times before the street-tough Will nearly lashes out but then breaks down in genuine acknowledgment of the statement's powerful, freeing truth. For good measure, he is assured twice more in the therapist's embrace: "It's not your fault. It's not your fault."

Additional resistance to forgetting comes in response to our more disingenuous attempts to put some form of it into practice. Despite the fact that it was repeated by one of the greatest nonviolent figures of all time (Mohandas K. Gandhi), I have never liked the saying, "Love the sinner, hate the sin."[64] It always seems those claiming to put it into practice are finally unable to maintain the distinction between person and act (as Gandhi seems to have been more capable of). And I've never known a person identified as the so-called "loved" sinner to feel particularly like an object of affection while others were busy hating some unapproved behavior. Allowing hate to be part of an equation where love also appears clearly lessens love in a way not intended. We don't always do well with holding such distinctions—love and hate, remembering and forgetting—in tension with one another.

The remembering of wrongdoing can have a similar effect on forgiving. It is not unusual to hear someone proclaim, "I can forgive you, but I will never forget." Thus, even an act of mercy can mask a sense of moral superiority and become a form of righteous retaliation that forever reminds the offender of his or her indebtedness. Making the case for forgetting, Volf points out that two things happen when these words are spoken:

> First, the gift of forgiveness is given in the dark wrapping paper of warning, even of threat. We keep score, and memories of transgressions become stockpiled like weapons during a cold war. And when the occasion arises, we use them to wage battle. In some cases, the memory of the offense seduces us into seeing dangers where none are lurking and justifying preventive strikes where no aggression against us is underfoot.
>
> Second, "I'll never forget" places on the offender an indelible sign that reads "Evildoer!" Once an offender, always an offender. Memory nails offenders' identities unalterably to their misdeeds. . . . the memory of the offense takes something away from what the forgiveness bestows.[65]

Even those who argue against forgetting acknowledge that the past is more of a threat than a promise.[66] Those who remain under moral judgment still have inherent worth as human beings, no matter how horrible their pasts, how heinous their deeds. To acknowledge the humanity of offenders through such expressions of regard may convey the possibility of mercy and forgiveness.[67] To suggest otherwise is to deny our own human capacity for evil. Less philosophically, those who have the threat of never forgetting held over their head may be understandably less inclined to seek forgiveness or reconciliation in the first place or ever again once seared by such an experience.

In whatever form, moving beyond the memory of injury, if at all possible, is not something to be pursued too quickly. What Volf has in mind is a forgetting that first "assumes that the matters of 'truth' and 'justice' have been taken care of."[68] If there is to be any kind of forgetting, it must always be on the other side of acknowledgment, forgiveness, reconciliation, healing, and transformation. In this sense, forgetting attends not only to the healing of the victim but the offender as well. The past is fully addressed with a future hope in mind. If forgiveness is a gift, then it is offered to the offender in the cancellation of guilt, the extension of love, the offering of relationship, and ultimately in the gift of innocence along the journey toward reconciliation.

## Non-remembering

We may not be able to determine whether intentional forgetting is possible or desirable, let alone healthy, moral, wise, or prudent. Outside of the complete context of a given event, interaction, or life story, it may not be helpful to suggest that forgetting is preferable to remembering, or vice-versa. Even if we take the possibility of forgetting seriously, we right away want to qualify the idea: Ahh, you mean "forgetting" (in quotes). Even Volf suggests that he is talking about "a certain kind of forgetting"[69] and argues for this possibility largely as a kind of theological "thought experiment" in the imagination of eternal possibilities in the world to come.

We get the idea that forgetting is really remembering in a certain kind of way. It is not "forgetting" that we put in quotes but rather "remembering" . . . remembering that allows forgetting, or, more accurately, what Volf calls "non-remembrance." Forgetting (as the inability to recall) is passive, unconscious, unintentional. Non-remembrance (as the ability to set aside) is active, fully aware, deliberate. Such non-remembering is only possible if we have first truthfully remembered the wrong suffered,

> integrated its memory into our life-story . . . dislodged [it] from the center of our identity and assigned a proper place on its periphery, and [broken] its hold over how we live in the present and how we project ourselves into the future.[70]

As a practical matter of forgiveness, forgetting means that the one who has suffered a wrong will no longer intentionally or otherwise bring that wrong to bear on the present. It says, "Although I make no guarantees that I will be able to forget what you've done and though we may both carry the scars for life, I refuse to let it stand between us."[71] Forgiving means that you don't act on the memory of the past and requires getting beyond certain moral emotions such as anger, shame, resentment and humiliation. These are considered "moral" because they necessarily involve judgment—of self and others. Thus, among other things, we are giving up the right to judge those who are blameworthy. This is liberating for both the offender and the victim.

Non-remembrance after forgiveness (or even reconciliation) is like forgiving after repentance. Remembering differently a forgiven offense may indeed be like forgiving a genuinely changed (i.e., different) person. We don't withhold forgiveness from a changed person just because there still exists within their new self a reminder of who they used to be and what they did, if only to us. Just as repentance is only possible because there has been wrongdoing, forgetting is only possible when we remember. We must remember to forget!

This is non-remembrance, a way of forgetting that which cannot be forgotten; non-remembering even painful memories without bitterness and hate; non-remembering in the only way that refuses to let our memories control us like a puppet of the past, that refuses to let our memories define us solely as victims or the other solely as offender (or vice-versa); non-remembering in grace and love.

If forgiveness is not disregard nor merely (and this is no small merely!) refusing to hate or exact revenge and is instead part of the attempt to genuinely love the wrongdoer, then we will—at least at first—love offenders despite what they did or who they were to us. Wishing offenders well, even loving them, is not born of an apathy of lost memory but of the same passionate memory out of which hate can emerge. As Gandhi also pointed out, it is not hate but indifference that is love's opposite. Perhaps the two are more closely related than we realize.[72] As an involuntary act, we cannot make ourselves forget any more than we can make ourselves fall asleep when not tired. But non-remembrance, in this sense, is something that can be learned, committed to, strived for as an active practice of forgiveness.

## FREEDOM FROM MEMORY'S HOLD

Most authors speak of memory almost exclusively in relation to the victim. How does this non-remembering apply to offenders? Aren't we already inclined to forget our trespasses too easily? Do we really need any encouragement? Should we suggest that offenders attempt forgetting or non-remembrance, even in the imagination or as some sort of experiment?

Perhaps some additional ideas would be useful. The most important may be that the offender should feel free to forget when—and only when—given permission by the victim to do so. For less serious slights we are accustomed to hearing someone genuinely say, "Hey, I've forgotten about it. You should too." Letting others know that we've chosen to remember in a different kind of way helps us to be accountable to that commitment. If the past unintentionally or unexpectedly brings itself to bear on the present in an unhealthy way, we invite others to call it to our attention where we may not see it.

This also prevents us from wielding the power of our victim status like an unchecked weapon. Elie Wiesel suggests that Jewish tradition requires forgiveness after being asked three times. After that, he says, we must ask forgiveness for not forgiving![73] There is nothing magical or inherently transformative about the number. (One can imagine its abuse by asking thrice in immediate succession.) Rather, the power in its offer of mutuality lies in the invitation to shift, to move beyond where one comfortably rests, to become unstuck, to grow. When we remember differently, we invite others to do so as well. When we are free, we invite others to also be free.

Out of consideration for the other, we may place our own liberation on hold if we believe the victim to still be burdened by the consequences of our actions. Katherine Power literally applied this precept to herself in the example mentioned in chapter three when she refused to accept the possibility of early release from prison out of concern for the victim's family. Conversely, to learn that others are free can be freeing to us.

Once so empowered, the offender might then take an additional, paradoxical step: ignore the invitation to forget and make every effort not to! No longer under the burden of "Remember!" enables forgetting to come through dedicated attempts to remember differently. This is a little like dealing with insomnia. Trying to stay awake to read or watch television will almost guarantee that I will soon be fast asleep. Additionally, making the effort to remember, whether invited to forget or not, prevents forgiveness or reconciliation from becoming one more burden for the victim couched in language of "getting past it," "finding closure," or carrying alone the responsibility to "never forget."

Remembering beyond the burden of someone else's "Remember!" means that, like the victim, the offender remembers rightly—actively, truthfully, deliberately, fully aware, in such way that the harm done takes its proper place in my identity, allowing me to break free from its hold over how I live in the present and how I hope for the future. This kind of merciful attitude, says Didier Pollefeyt, accompanied by a proper emphasis on justice, keeps us from reducing the offender to a single moment of his or her existence.[74]

We forget as we remember differently. We remember differently as we forget. Remembering and forgetting, embraced together. Each made possible because of the other, as gifts to Self and the Other. Both making possible forgiveness. Perhaps another way of understanding what Jesus meant when he said, "Do this in remembrance of me."

Our exploration of the complex considerations of justice confronts us with some emerging paradoxes of forgiveness:

- Forgiveness frees the other person from the burden of justice over an injury for which forgiveness is only possible because of its demand that justice be done.
- Forgiveness insists that a situation has been made right which cannot be made right.
- Forgiveness proclaims that nothing is owed for a debt that cannot be repaid.
- Forgiveness releases from guilt the conscience that cannot be freed.
- Forgiveness forgets that which cannot be forgotten.

## Chapter 5

# THE PRACTICE OF FORGIVENESS

Forgiveness is difficult. It is hard work, risky, demanding. And like theologian Dietrich Bonhoeffer's notion of grace, it is costly not cheap. But we have also said that forgiveness can be simple and, at least for some even seems—dare we say?—easy. Some people just seem to be naturally more forgiving or less inclined to take offense or be sensitive to injury or injustice. Others' emotional health and maturity provides a solid existing foundation for engaging an offender with love and empathy. Still others let their moral compass, directed by the community in which they live, guide them to gracious action without denying, minimizing, or setting aside key issues of concern.

One woman mentioned earlier, whose son was lost in the tragic events of 9-11, found forgiveness difficult because she faced unresolved legal, emotional, and moral dilemmas all at once. That each of these "domains" of our lives can be an integral part of our experience of forgiveness speaks to the complexity. That they come together in unique ways may help to determine whether forgiveness is easier, more difficult, or even possible. For the Amish who quickly forgave the murder of their precious children as recounted in chapter two, no single factor stood in the way of the other. The genuineness of forgiveness that comes so easily is questioned by those of us whose dysfunctional relationships, demands for rights, or isolated moral teachings may unwittingly prevent us from putting the very principles and beliefs we claim to value into practice.

We've ventured into and through the complexity of forgiveness. I'm also interested in exploring what makes something that can be so difficult seem to come so easily for some. Perhaps the rest of us can learn from this how to make forgiveness more a part of our lives, our world. Our reflection ought to be connected to our action. In the graduate Peacemaking and Conflict Studies program in which I teach, we always keep in mind the importance of balancing theory (reflection) with practice (action). Each is important, and we should be careful about merely reflecting abstractly on certain things without practising them, and about practising certain things without reflecting "theoretically" on them. But it's not just that we try to provide both in equal (but separate) measures. Rather, we encourage students to work at these tasks integratively as reflective practitioners. What is the significance of this work?

## A PEACEMAKING PRACTICE

I like the metaphor of practice and think it can be helpful to us here. By definition, *practise* is what practitioners do. While living in Canada I got used to seeing the word spelled with an "s" (as in that last sentence). Following more British conventions of English, the spelling is used to distinguish between use of the word as a verb and as a noun (with a "c"). As a verb, practising is what we do to learn something. As a noun, we may seek to develop a practice at which we want to become skilled or proficient. And though we say "practice makes perfect," one must necessarily practise imperfectly at something before one can get close to perfecting it. We may never become perfect, but both concepts together help us to understand the connection between what we do and who we are.

In his important study on morality and virtue, Alasdair MacIntyre has defined a practice as any form of . . . cooperative activity through which goods internal to that form of activity are realized in the course of trying to achieve those standards of excellence which are appropriate to, and partly definitive of, that form of activity.[75]

While forgiveness may achieve many "goods" external to its practice (from improved health for self to reconciliation with another), such benefits may be had in other ways and pursued for one's own good. And as we have seen, the "rules" that serve as the standards of excellence for good forgiveness practice (for example, the necessary elements for apology and justice) may be informal (i.e., unwritten) or even tacit (not consciously formulated). Practices such as forgiveness, claims MacIntyre, require both "the exercise of [acquired] technical skills" and "a certain kind of relationship between those who participate in it" that "can only be elaborated and possessed within an ongoing [moral and] social tradition."[76]

This suggests that forgiveness has intrinsic value and not only requires a certain virtuousness before its practice but is capable of evoking virtue in individuals. Forgiveness holds the potential to create among those who pursue its shared practice—whether intentional or not—a community in which forgiveness is the norm. In this sense the practice of forgiveness provides a political alternative to punishment and other forms of violence.

How can these notions of practice/practise help us go beyond the limited and limiting understandings and practices of forgiveness so frequently summarized in abstract principles and ungrounded steps?

Contrary to most other works on forgiveness with which I am familiar, I have largely tried to avoid saying how forgiveness *should* be understood, how forgiveness *should* be defined, how it *should* be practised. Instead I have described what we do, how we understand forgiveness, the meanings it has, and how it is practised. For Christians, forgiveness—particularly what seem to be its extraordinary expressions—is often unwittingly portrayed as an unreachable ideal we can't possibly live up to, rather than as an everyday practice of discipleship. Among other ways in which this is done, ethicist Glen Stassen has noted how Christians have historically confused the Beatitudes in Jesus' Sermon on the Mount (including those pertaining to forgiveness) with such impossibly high ideals as can only be reached by "straining toward impossible standards of perfection."[77]

I introduce one of my undergraduate courses on peacemaking by reading the beatitude, "Blessed are the peacemakers, for they will be called children of God." Then I ask, "How many of you think of yourselves as peacemakers?" A few hands are raised. "Well, one way to understand this verse," I continue, "is that only those who are peacemakers will be considered God's children." Downcast looks. Then I ask, "Now, how many of you consider yourselves to be a child of God?" Most, if not all, hands go up. "Well," I continue, "perhaps another way to understand this verse is that all those who consider themselves God's children are called to be peacemakers. Let's see what that means together."

With that suggestion, I invite them to join me on a journey which is first one of recognition. As only a small percentage of my students come from the Anabaptist tradition, they (and too often my Mennonite Brethren students as well) see themselves as outside the Peace Church tradition. I draw a continuum on the board to illustrate how, between the oversimplified extremes of "Silence" and "Violence" as ways of being in the world, most would not identify themselves solely on either end. In fact, it is more likely that we find ourselves at various points along the continuum in relation to different issues: for war and against abortion, against the death penalty and for assisted suicide, and so forth.

Even as I encourage them to develop a consistent approach to such issues, I offer an inclusive model that promotes dialogue between those standing at different places and invites them to recognize themselves as already on the way, as already practising some form of peacemaking. If they can't see that, then they are not likely to think of themselves as peacemakers because they have been led to believe that only the most difficult of tasks, the highest of ideals, qualify them as such.

There is no other place to start, they think, than to love (and forgive) the likes of Osama bin Laden; conscientious objection to war; tax resistance against all forms of violence. These seem not only impossible but also tend to invalidate or minimize any "lesser" act of love or forgiveness as a form (or practice) of peacemaking. Then, if they hear the word *peace* elsewhere, they steer clear of those who use it.

And so, as a more inclusive alternative, we continue through the semester to practise anger management, mediation, and negotiation. Eventually we come around to reflecting on how we can respond nonviolently to injustice in the world, looking to Gandhi and Martin Luther King Jr., and other lesser known figures, as models for practice. Some go on to learn the Victim-Offender Reconciliation Process in another course and mediate an actual criminal case, not only observing but helping to foster forgiveness between victim and offender. They may continue in yet another course to engage the "bigger" issues of peace: injustice, oppression, violence, war. Without intending to, or even recognizing it, they are practising peace, becoming peacemakers beyond their initial limited, and aggrandized, understandings.

## PRACTISING THE PRACTICE OF FORGIVENESS

As Kraybill, Nolt, and Weaver-Zercher have suggested, "forgiveness probably comes easier for the Amish than it does for most Americans."[78] If so, it's not that practising forgiveness is easy because the Amish don't bother with the necessary and hard work of giving deep and thoughtful consideration to its complexities. That would be an unfair and simplistic assessment. Rather, they've moved beyond the complexities to the simplicity of forgiveness made possible by "a three-hundred-year-old tradition [of practising] love of enemies and the forgiveness of offenders."[79] The Amish don't have to go through the difficult process of deciding whether to forgive in any given instance because, after three hundred years of practice, even something as complex as forgiveness has become a habitual part of the group's cultural "repertoire of beliefs and behaviors."[80]

But even the Amish practice of forgiveness should not be held out as an ideal, unless in this way: as a lesson about the value of practise. After all, no single Amish individual has been practising forgiveness for three hundred years! But, as Kraybill, Nolt, and Weaver-Zercher point out, daily life and practise is informed by that history and culture and gives the Amish "a head start on forgiveness long before an offense ever occurs."[81]

We sometimes say we are "just practising" to convey that we are not trying as hard as we might if we were performing as well as we are really able. There is that (unfortunate) sense of the word. None of us would go to a doctor who practises medicine or an attorney who practises law if we felt they were merely using us to prepare for real patient care or even to sharpen their less-than-adequate skills. Some may not even have the courage to go to a hair stylist in training! But neither would we seek the services of a doctor or lawyer who, having established a practice, never practises! I like that sense of the word and know its importance. Having tried for many years, and not very successfully still, to learn a second language, I know that what is not practised quickly slips away. "Use it or lose it," we say. Perhaps that is what has happened to those who are part of the Christian faith tradition but see the Amish practice of forgiveness as extraordinary.

Even different theories of practice recognize the progressive nature of learning. We don't practice the most difficult things first. If forgiveness is difficult for most of us, where do we begin? We know about the tendency of such practices as hatred, vengeance, and violence to feed into themselves, creating an unending cycle and escalating spiral that seems to take on a life of its own. We almost don't have to try, don't need to practise. We less recognize such practices as empathy, forgiveness, and reconciliation as having a similar character. But perhaps we have already begun unknowingly.

A friend who once led a very different life in his past said to me, "I sometimes marvel at how foreign those old behaviors now are to me, and how much a part of me are those things that I once knew nothing about." When I asked him how the change came about, he seemed almost surprised by the question, as if he hadn't thought about it before. The things he had in mind weren't brought about by a program or steps with an identifiable starting point, he said, although he had determined at various times to move away from his prior practices and grow in other directions. "I guess just being a part of this group that acts like this all the time," he said, referring to his church community.

This is why Celestin Musekura argues that the impact of believers who attempt to "live out their faith publicly [and] come into contact with the harsh realities of brokenness and despair" in society "will greatly depend on the ability to develop disciplines that bind its members into a holy communion characterized by the practices of love, embrace, and forgiveness."[82]

This is a communal exploration of the practice of forgiveness that goes beyond individualistic and therapeutic approaches, practised not only within communities but between themselves and others within larger society as an alternative to dealing with collective transgressions, mediating social forgiveness, and promoting the reconciliation of enemies. In a world filled with tribal and ethnic conflict and even genocide, this may prove more challenging and complex than individual forgiveness but such "communities of forgiveness" may be the best place for individuals to integrate forgiveness practices into their daily lives and where collective and even socio-political forgiveness may be initiated.[83]

## THE DOING AND BEING OF FORGIVENESS

The journey of my students, the grace of the Amish, and the realization of my friend remind me of two stories. I told of the first in an earlier book:

> In the sermon he preached at his father's funeral, Stanley Hauerwas reflected on his father's lifelong gentleness. That his father's gentleness "was so effortless," he wrote, "helps us better understand Jesus' Beatitudes." They are not, as we typically think

of them, ideals we must strive to attain. Rather, those who answer the call to follow Jesus will find themselves becoming meeker, or poorer in spirit, and better peacemakers. Who we are as Christians will transform what we do.[84]

As with the Amish experience, we might identify that simply as "socialization," which is clearly not limited to religious communities. But that is less a cause for dismissal because of its irrelevance to us as individuals than an important lesson about the place of communities for learning practices such as forgiveness. Like any difficult practice, it cannot be understood or practised in isolation. Communities of practice, as Etienne Wenger calls them, develop a shared repertoire of resources that include experiences, stories, tools, and ways of addressing problems that emerge over time.[85]

If the larger Christian community has anything to learn from the Amish, it's that we have failed to be the kind of (countercultural) communities that embody love, forgiveness, and reconciliation. We have left ourselves without the shared repertoire of resources necessary for practising them. With the abundance of theological explorations available on forgiveness, and its roots in the Judeo-Christian tradition, it cannot be that a lack of understanding of forgiveness or even conviction about its rightness is primarily the problem for most Christians; an alternative explanation must be that we lack the cultivation of skills made possible through the regular practice of forgiveness. Practice simply does not permeate all of our thought and life.

There is an additional element shared by Hauerwas' story and my friend's experience that comes from significant involvement in a community of practice and the practising of its practices: the formation of identity. We recognize that what we *do* transforms who we *are*. A fairy tale by Max Beerbohm illustrates this well:

A man who lived a life of great wickedness and misery is captivated by the beauty and grace of a young actress he encounters at an opera. The sharp piercing of unexpected love to his hardened heart is as unfamiliar as it is overwhelming to the man. He immediately petitions her as a privileged lord for her hand in marriage.

Alas, in her response he learns that she could never be his bride, for she cannot imagine giving her love to any man with a face such as his—tarnished with the evil and vanity that had characterized his life up until that very moment.

Despondent nearly to the point of suicide, the man encounters a mask maker with a magical ability to fashion waxen masks not only of great beauty but of saintly countenance. He finds and is fitted with just such a mask that perfectly mirrors the true love he feels for the young women.

The man's great desire is realized, and in an encounter that forges a genuine and sacred love, they devote themselves to one another for life. As part of this new life together, the man sets aside his lordly wealth in an act of true penitence as an atonement and sacrifice to cleanse his soul of the evil wrought by his previous life. Together they retreat to a village where their days are filled with joy and simplicity, though the man's past still lingers, making him ever wary of its long shadow.

One day, as they are setting out to celebrate the anniversary of their marriage, a woman not only familiar with his earlier life of debauchery but a participant in it, with an evil face of her own, recognizes the man despite his marvelous new visage. Set on exposing the man to his bride, she reveals his past and with poisonous venom begs, "In honor of our old friendship, show me one last time the face I once caressed, the lips that were so sweet to me! Remove your mask and I will leave."

The man refuses, moving menacingly toward the evil woman. "Hypocrite! Liar! False saint!" she cries out, "then I will unmask you."

She springs at him and claws at the waxen mask, tearing it from his face. The man stands motionless in humiliation and despair, knowing that his secret has been exposed. All is lost. Not even his wife would pardon such a hypocrite. He hangs his head in shame.

But his wife gazes at him, bewildered by his response. For his life of genuine repentance has transformed his face to a glory far surpassing the mask behind which he has hidden for so long.[86]

Augsburger summarizes the lessons of Beerbohm's story well: "What begins with joining a new community leads to a radical shift in values and behavior, and then in appearance, resulting in a transformation of the core person and personality."[87] Perhaps not as dramatically as this fictional story presents, my friend mentioned above experienced this same radical shift. Gandhi captured the many dimensions of this transformational process well, noting that our thoughts become our words, our words become our behaviors, our behaviors become our habits, our habits become our values, and our values become our destiny.[88] We understand words, behaviors, and habits as sets of practices; values as part of character and virtue; and destiny as wrapped up in our community of identity.

But this "becoming" is not passive; we are not without agency in our own transformation. Before we become persons of forgiving character or forgiving persons, we practise acts of forgiveness.

## BEYOND PRACTISE: THE ART OF FORGIVENESS

Until we find ourselves in a situation where it is difficult to forgive, we may not realize that offenses—especially when committed against us—present new things to think about and deal with; we may not have anticipated how limited our capacity to imagine ways to make things right can become; how powerful emotional forces can stand in our way; how difficult it is to put even the most strongly held beliefs into practice. Not recognizing the complexity of the difficulty (or, the difficulty of the complexity), we are not fully aware of how demanding, risky, or costly forgiveness can be.

The process of learning new skills can be thought of in terms of a sequence involving the interaction of two dimensions: *consciousness* (or awareness) and *competence* (or ability). There are four possible ways in which these two aspects may be related when it comes to dealing with conflict and learning to forgive.

The first is that we are *unconsciously incompetent*; that is, we don't know what we don't know. While each of us is skilled in some important ways based on our own experience that includes both successes and failures, we may simply not be aware of how unskilled we truly are. For example, I've found that many students of conflict (and people in general) think that they are good listeners. This perception is challenged when I plunge my students into their first active listening exercise. They recognize that in some ways we are all "blissfully ignorant"; I encourage them to be open to identifying what it is that they don't yet know. This represents a shift toward *conscious incompetence*, identifying areas in which we need to learn and develop new skills.

As we practice in the relative safety of the classroom where our mistakes have significantly smaller consequences than in the real world, we recognize areas for growth and our confidence slowly builds as we commit to the journey. We progress to more difficult practices, from mediation to negotiation to forgiveness. As the semester moves on, "Aha!" moments are experienced; what wasn't thought possible is now recognized as something that can be done, something that *is* being done—though sometimes after the fact ("I did it!"). This is *conscious competence*, a recognition and celebration of our success. Though often quite effective, one can often see the effort on the faces of those persons acting with intention, much like the golfer working to insert a new technique into her swing or a second language learner putting words together with the proper syntax. The seemingly effortless smoothness of a professional's swing or the beauty of a native spoken accent may be missing even if the ball is going farther and the words are understandable.

Only continued practice can move us to the next station of our journey. Here what started unrecognized and later reflected so much effort now begins to become part of what we do and who we are. *Unconscious competence*. We have returned to being unaware but now no longer of our incompetence; we are competently resolving disputes, making peace, forgiving others and opening ourselves up to being forgiven. And, like the Amish, to others around us our actions look (deceptively) effortless, intuitive, like "second nature." Forgiveness as practised technique becomes artistry.[89]

## On Confusion

I can be pessimistic by nature. That may seem a bit contradictory for someone deeply interested in forgiveness, especially since, as I suggested earlier, having a sense of (optimistic) hope is one of the most important attributes of a peacemaker. Pessimism does not position me well, especially as an attitude born of cynicism.[90] However, I have tried to overcome the most negative effects of that perspective while retaining its benefits by embracing a phrase attributed to Italian political theorist Antonio Gramsci: "Pessimism of the intellect, optimism of the will."

As I think, I tend to see, anticipate, or emphasize possible negative or undesirable outcomes. However, as I act, I do so with a disposition toward looking on the more positive side of events or conditions and expecting the best outcomes. The intellectual critique I regularly bring to situations or ideas often means that I see possibilities others haven't even thought of. At its best, I am often able to call attention to potential pitfalls or anticipate problems that can then be addressed and avoided up front. I often surprise my colleagues by affirming their proposals after subjecting them to a rigorous round of questioning. Pessimism of the intellect, optimism of the will: a combination requiring something like what Martin Luther King Jr. called being tough-minded and tender-hearted.[91] Judgment and grace.

This reflection on forgiveness has been in part an exercise of pessimism, with challenges and complexities unflinchingly noted along the way. Perhaps in that sense it has been more of a journey for the confused, where problems and difficulties affirm what is already recognized as hard about forgiveness, and an attitude of constructive pessimism serves as a reality check to ensure that change essential for genuine forgiveness is not superficial.[92] I have not provided simple steps or answers to the questions raised at the outset. But I have tried to embrace the confusion of difficult questions and go beyond pessimism to affirm a way through the complexity, perhaps even suggesting an answer to the question that has not yet been asked about how one forgives: by becoming more forgiving! And how does one do that? By forgiving.

It is not much of an answer, circular and paradoxical at best. But perhaps it is the only answer, certainly clearer now that we have worked our way through some of the complexities of forgiveness than if I had offered it at the start. It reflects the hopeful optimism that what is difficult can be done once started, even if only the most basic elements are practised at the outset. Regret becomes an apology. A reluctant offer of forgiveness leads to full reparation. We practise these things according to our own understanding (how else?), by engaging the practices of others in their own understanding and creating new meaning in and from our experience together.

As something discovered in this way, forgiveness suggests that something about the process—its timing or place or method or its degree—is unexpected, even if one sets out intentionally on a journey of healing, forgiveness, or reconciliation. One knows not when or where or how, or even if, it may come about. That doesn't mean that forgiveness can't happen; only that it can't be made to happen, no matter how much one practises.

*Chapter 6*

# BEYOND FORGIVENESS

A book is not typically written like it is read—from front to back, chapters in order, perhaps over a relatively short period of time. This book is no exception. It likely took longer than its length suggests. Later chapters were completed before earlier ones, material from one chapter moved to another with still further reorganizing (and rewriting) again later; the writing of one chapter flowed into the next without pause, with others thought about almost endlessly before they could be started.

Beginning this last chapter has been particularly difficult. More can always be written, additional research can always be done, other important aspects could be addressed in still more chapters. It's the curse of the academic. I was not even sure this would be the final chapter, but it is.

In reviewing the many books written on our topic, it seems not only typical but assumed that a book on forgiveness most appropriately ends with an exploration of reconciliation as the ultimate expression of personal and social peace where forgiveness might (some say should) lead. After all, what else could be meant by "beyond forgiveness"?

This is not a chapter on reconciliation. Although the title indeed suggests that we move beyond forgiveness along our journey to something else, I mean it in a different sense. All along I've encouraged us to look beyond the more limiting ideas and understandings of forgiveness, and I want to continue along that pathway, not end it at some greater outcome to which forgiveness merely leads.[93]

## The Problems of Forgiveness

While one of my purposes is to explore, and understand, and even value forgiveness, I have not idolized its practice. Forgiveness is far too important to resort to uncritical oversimplification or promotion. Rather, I want to remind the reader one last time of the complexity of forgiveness and suggest ways through. I do this first in the form of reflecting on several problems of forgiveness not yet directly discussed: the personal problem, the cultural problem, and—elaborating on the above—what I call the reconciliation problem.[94] Each reflects a particular challenge embedded in other issues I have discussed along the way, but each also has its own unique set of meanings worth addressing separately, however briefly.

### The personal problem

At one point or another, everyone feels hurt, misunderstood, taken advantage of, even victimized. The reasons for harm are many, and at least some minor transgression is a normal part of all relationships.

As mentioned, all of us have our own dispositions in reacting to injury, often shaped by the experiences of life and the emotional ledgers, or scales, that balance the credits and debits of relationships past and present. We might reasonably expect individuals to act according their characters, though—given the many challenges faced in considering forgiveness—even the slightest change in circumstances may make the difference between forgiveness offered or withheld, accepted or rejected.

In this sense, the human capacity to forgive (and be forgiven) is based on an internal orientation or process that takes account of injustices not only in relation to present offences but is deeply informed by one's personal history of making things right (or not) with others, primarily in one's family of origin.[95] Organizations, institutions, even countries, have a kind of corporate or national character—as weak or strong, punitive or conciliatory—with a shared history denying or accepting of collective guilt or responsibility, that orients them in similar ways to forgiveness.

John Patton notes the central role in this process of guilt and shame and the defenses used by persons to spare themselves the difficult experience of these powerful emotions.[96] Each of these defenses—resentment, rage, power, self-righteousness—are likely to be even more salient in settings of conflict and create problems for persons struggling with forgiveness if their role, which is often hidden, is not realized. Because of this, what seems like a minor, even petty offense can trigger a disproportionate demand for justice and compensation beyond the particulars of the current transgression.

Another important dimension of this internal (intra-personal, intra-group) problem is the question of forgiving one's self. Many feel that dealing with conflicts and offenses between depends significantly on our ability to deal with those within.

We are not isolated individuals. Thus, we don't discover our own need for forgiveness outside of the context of reflecting on relationships with others, where injury and brokenness inevitably occur. Forgiving self is difficult when one has not experienced forgiveness by others or when harm done to us is has not been recognized or made right.

In the case of the latter, the lack of resolution or understanding of the reasons for the offense against us can lead to overwhelming feelings of oppressive guilt when our only recourse is to blame ourselves. Not forgiving ourselves can come from the inability to get beyond a sense of self largely defined by the unresolved injuries we have suffered or committed, even (or perhaps, especially) if we don't walk around thinking of our self in that way.

One key to forgiving is gaining an understanding of and empathy toward the other. When I have been harmed, honest self-reflection may lead to the realization that I am more like the offender than I am different; not "There but for the grace of God go I," but rather, "There I go too!" Appropriate feelings of guilt—defined as a set of behavioral controls internalized within the conscience—represent acceptance of responsibility for our failures in life. Understood this way, guilt is seen "as a potentially good and redemptive force rooted in responsibility and leading to repentance and growth."[97] However, without understanding and accepting that who we are is not solely defined by what we have done in one instance, we may not be able to overcome unrealistic feelings of guilt for not living up to our own or others' expectations and can allow feelings of deserved punishment to prevent self-forgiveness.

When I have committed an offense, I may be forced to reconcile the (good) person I believe myself to be with the (bad) one who has harmed another. A proper degree of shame—understood as mechanisms of discretionary controls externalized before others—is important for relating rightly to a fully integrated sense of self that experiences both good and bad as part of the whole person.

But this can be particularly difficult when a loving act of mercy toward me in the form of "undeserved" forgiveness only serves as yet another reminder of my failure. Anderson argues that such love can be like a millstone around our neck and suggests that those who betray "do not need forgiveness that issues from the love of another, but the restoration of a love within themselves that has gone awry."[98]

In such experiences of disgrace, shame can be a disorienting feeling of exposure, humiliation, and an alienating exclusion from one's community. Understanding shame's positive role in our life in relating to others helps us to discern what is good about ourselves so that we may more freely accept responsibility for where we've fallen short. In this sense, shame has the potential of reminding one of the deep valuing of self (apart from behavior), community belonging and inclusion, concern for relationship, and hope for the future.[99]

Robert Coles captures this overall process of learning to forgive both self and others best in noting the need to understand the mistakes and errors of our ways, in the hope that we can do (can be) better; and forgive ourselves, lest we give our errant or evil side the continuing hold over us that such a refusal of forgiveness all too commonly, readily ensures.[100]

Thus, the "personal problem" of forgiveness involves the connection between forgiving self and forgiving others, significantly shaped by our history of making things right with others (including things being made right with us), and each contributing to a sense of identity as forgiving of others and deserving to be forgiven by others. Here, shame and guilt (both overt and covert processes, depending on the cultural context) are necessary and important emotions in their positive form and "contribute to and find resolution in authentic forgiveness and the experience of grace."[101]

## THE CULTURAL PROBLEM

These powerful personal factors are also shaped by an even wider context in which one's response to injury carries conscious and unconscious social and cultural influences. When one's social setting is characterized by a spiraling cycle of violence and revenge, the remembering of the injustices against one's group—big or small—may also pass from one generation to the next in ways that erase from memory examples of mercy and forgiveness and perpetuate actions catalyzed by hurtful accounts of the past.[102] This has been seen in such places as Northern Ireland, the Middle East, and between countless other ethnic groups around the world.

In his short essay on forgiveness (see note 56), French philosopher Jacques Derrida asserts that the language of forgiveness, rooted in the Abrahamic faith tradition, has been adapted and globalized to all people and cultures, even those without European or 'biblical' origins.[103] This process of adoption and adaptation has resulted in a wide diversity of understandings and practices of forgiveness. According to Derrida, this can lead to confusions which diminish the meaning of forgiveness. But, when properly understood, there is much to be gained from their consideration as well.

As mentioned in chapter one, nearly every discussion of forgiveness includes a list of things that forgiveness is not. Forgiveness is not forgetting. Forgiveness does not minimize wrongdoing. Forgiveness is not something that can be offered on behalf of others. Forgiveness is not the same thing as reconciliation, etc. Making such distinctions can be helpful in setting aside misconceptions that make forgiveness seem too easy or too difficult or fail to distinguish it from other things such as reconciliation. However, each of these aspects is understood and valued differently by people whose history, culture, and religion—to name only a few factors—influence their experience and understanding of forgiveness. So the essence of this particular forgiveness "problem" is first a definitional problem.

David Augsburger identifies a set of dominant cultural polarities of responses to perceived wrongdoing that provides an alternative to understanding forgiveness as an either-or, absolute concept.[104] This provides us with a lens for seeing the many "faces" of forgiveness in the tension between actions that seek to maintain relationships and those that sever relationships. While some responses, such as revenge and ostracization, are universally understood as divisive, and others such as acceptance and excusing are likewise understood as unifying, each has its cost and benefit and suggests a variety of forms or types of forgiveness based on centrally accepted cultural values (for example, the valuing of harmony calling for a "forgiveness of overlooking," honor for a "forgiveness of repayment,"and so forth).

In Simon Wiesenthal's *The Sunflower*, Nechama Tec notes that forgiveness has "many gradations" and, similarly, "non-forgiveness may [also] come in a variety of shadings."[105] Tec's observation suggests that the responses to injury, and perhaps the outcomes, are almost unlimited. We understand almost all forms of forgiveness as imperfect, limited, or partial responses along a spectrum between unconditional acceptance of the other and the unwavering demand for justice. Only the most imaginative and committed of efforts on the part of both parties will make it possible to transform extreme expressions of denial and anger—from passive resignation to revenge—for finding true forgiveness.

Thus, the "cultural problem" of forgiveness is concerned with our basic understanding of what it is and how it works in and between communities—authentically, inclusively, and meaningfully among people with diverse experiences of healing broken relationships.

## THE RECONCILIATION PROBLEM

Given the great condition of brokenness in our world, one can clearly justify a preference, even a bias, for reconciliation as primary for mediators, counselors, pastors, and activists; theologians, social scientists, and philosophers; peacemaking practitioners and scholars of all kind. Reconciliation, some argue, provides the necessary context for the responsible practice of forgiveness as more than simply "a social lubricant, a survival technique, a relational strategy, a memory fatigue, an individual escape, a dismissal of hurt or anger or a ritual of denial."[106]

Kraus argues that the idea of reconciliation—closely associated with repentance and forgiveness—is "[a]t the core of peacemaking."[107] According to Kraus, the goal of forgiveness as illustrated by Jesus "is reconciliation and restoration of peace between alienated parties."[108] Martin Luther King Jr., that great reconciler and lover of enemies, went even further, making no distinction between the two: "Forgiveness," he said, "means reconciliation."[109] The connection is worth giving serious attention.

With our ever-improving capacity to perpetrate violence more efficiently and more effectively, one should be grateful that reconciliation is increasingly recognized as an important political process of peacebuilding.[110] MacIntyre suggests that the solution to such political problems requires the practice of virtues (and institutions which will sustain them), the central one exhibited in forgiveness being charity. Communities in which the inherent good of such practices is achieved, says MacIntyre, are communities of reconciliation.[111]

Forgiveness provides an opportunity for reconciliation by offering the possibility of a new future. At the very least, suggests South African Archbishop Desmond Tutu, even if we cannot know the future, forgiveness is a statement about what we wish to leave behind: grudges, resentment, bitterness, injustice, violence.[112] That is to be valued on its own. In Bishop Tutu's words, "There can be no future without it."

However, forgiveness does not always lead to reconciliation even if reconciliation almost always includes some degree or type of forgiveness.[113] That may suggest the relative importance of forgiveness and make the case that the responsible practice of reconciliation should not allow forgiveness to become a means to its own end (even if one disagrees that it must have another means, namely reconciliation, beyond itself).

Further, the outcome-oriented ideal of reconciliation contains the prevailing image of agreement as solution (i.e., a signed document), thus creating "the expectation that the conflict has ended."[114] Such a view reinforces the idea of forgiveness as one-time event we've tried to overcome here.

Addressing reconciliation as part of or emerging from forgiveness also raises additional questions related to truth, justice, and mercy.[115] These were discussed at some length in chapter four. Without rejecting a preference for healing, restoration, or reconciliation, and without accepting the equally untenable notion of neutrality of orientation toward outcome, I simply want to propose that forgiveness, not reconciliation, be the last topic in a book about . . . forgiveness.

How does one speak to the healing of broken relationships, the reconciling of adversaries, and the embracing of enemies without diminishing that which has come before? How can one discuss the powerful experience of reconciliation as the ultimate manifestation of peacemaking without minimizing the significance and the great complexity of forgiveness, without reducing forgiveness to a prelude to something even greater? Whether conflating the two processes or privileging the objective of reconciliation above forgiveness, this is the "reconciliation problem" I seek to avoid here.

At several other places before this chapter I used the metaphor of *beyond* to help us think about going further than some of the more popular, accepted, or traditional ways of understanding forgiveness. Beyond apology. Beyond memory. Beyond forgiveness. Having discussed above some of the additional problems of forgiveness, it is time now to get beyond some of these issues to some final thoughts.

## SIMPLE AND COMPLEX

At Fresno Pacific University, our incoming freshmen and transfer students take a course which introduces them to key issues of the Christian faith and a life of discipleship, particularly from an Anabaptist perspective. For many, this is their first in-depth foray into biblical and theological topics beyond a more basic "Sunday school approach." This can be a rewarding, though potentially perilous, pathway as they discover the complexities of such things as the Bible and church history that up until that time they have understood in more basic ways.

I note that this can be a potentially troubling experience because, if not properly guided, the students may allow some of the questions raised in the course to weaken rather than strengthen their faith. The key to this process lies in getting to what theologian Karl Barth and philosopher Paul Ricoeur refer to as the second naiveté. Ricoeur and Barth argue that we must first go beyond an unreflective approach to the text that merely sees the Bible as an ahistorical, disembodied personal message from God. Such an uncritical approach to the text is not likely to lead the reader beyond what he or she already believes and practices.

However, a second danger lies in the necessary deconstructing process of such criticism that distances the reader from the text without providing a way "back" or "through" to understandings that give our relationship to God new meaning. Barth and Ricoeur believed that such an engagement ought to lead beyond a preoccupation with examining the topic or subject (the Bible, faith, etc.) and into a new kind of encounter with God. This encounter is made possible by gaining a so-called second naiveté that allows the reader, now equipped with deeper, more complex understandings of the text, to re-enter it with a different kind of simplicity and be transformed in ways not previously possible.

Our graduate students have a similar experience in our Peacemaking and Conflict Studies program. While not necessarily guided by the divine, it is important to their understanding of conflict—particularly in preventing what we sometimes refer to as "the paralysis of analysis" which complexity can lead to.

As one of the more theoretically oriented courses in our program, my Conflict Analysis class introduces the students to the more subtle dynamics and complexities of conflicts. Going beyond some of the more basic understandings of earlier courses—the roles of victim and offender, the distinction between process and content, the significance of constructive versus unconstructive participation—students explore the sometimes contradictory alliances of adversaries and friends. They study ways that process can become a substantive issue in a conflict, and the importance of understanding power in the dynamics of human interaction, particularly its systemic dimensions in determining who gets to set the rules and decide what counts as "cooperative" or "unhelpful."

However, like the deconstructing process of critical biblical hermeneutics, this new awareness can leave students feeling that, with so many factors to be considered, it is impossible to know where to begin in dealing with and getting to some kind of transformation of the conflict. "Do what you already know how to do," I tell them, "but now do so with a different set of ears and eyes, paying attention to the more subtle and complex dynamics as you apply your new analytic tools along with your most basic peacemaking understandings and skills."

These experiences illustrate an important principle in the idea of practicing forgiveness beyond understanding. The principle has to do with balancing simplicity with complexity; or, as illustrated in the examples above, going from more simplistic understandings through complexity and into a new kind of simplicity. This is what United States

Supreme Court Justice Oliver Wendell Holmes meant when he said, "I would not give a fig for the simplicity this side of complexity, but I would give my life for the simplicity on the other side of complexity." It's the same principle that once prompted the sophisticated Swiss-German theologian Karl Barth to a very simple, yet profound, response. When asked about his greatest theological insight from all his years and many volumes of work, he offered, "Jesus loves me, this I know, for the Bible tells me so!"[116]

## CONCLUSION

Forgiveness is complex. It is also simple. We understand how admonitions such as "Forgive and forget," "Say you're sorry," "Just let go," and nearly countless others can come across as an overly simplistic—and unhelpful—understanding and application of complex dynamics, at least at first glance. In his book, *The Moral Imagination*, John Paul Lederach argues that peacebuilding activities—in which forgiveness might have some place—are undertaken within complex systems with an array of actors advancing processes at multiple levels all at the same time.[117] Once the fuller complexity of such activities is understood and embraced in all its "multiplicity, interdependency, and simultaneity" he suggests, one can identify a core set of patterns and dynamics that serve as the basic elements of peacebuilding.

On this side of examining some of the complexities involved in forgiveness, we can now look back at our discussion. Instead of suggesting we have comprehensively covered all possible dynamics from every perspective (or even dealt with forgiveness exhaustively from a single perspective), the topics of our chapters can perhaps be said to reflect the basic elements, or—as Lederach suggests about peacebuilding[118]—"essences" of forgiveness. These include injury and hurdles to mending relationships; the subtle dynamics of apology; inwardly reflective and externally interactive processes and practices for healing and making things right.

We have looked at what people do and feel and say along the pathway between injury and discovering forgiveness, but we have not reduced forgiveness (nor our understanding of it) to specific rules, prescribed steps, or even broader principles. We have identified those things that can prevent or allow for the possibility of forgiveness, but we have not succumbed to the false dualism that pronounces this or that attitude or act as fitting (or not) within a prescribed definition for what counts as "real" forgiveness.

We have explored through examples the significance of certain types of interaction between victims and offenders without ignoring the many meanings that people give to their own reality of injury, victimization, healing, and forgiveness. And we have encountered the possibility of a wide range of consequences to breaches in human relationships but have not assumed the gracious and often beautiful experience of reconciliation—or even forgiveness, as the ideal outcome for every situation.

Amid seeking to avoid narrow and limiting categories, our exploration suggests that the "essences" of forgiveness are not even best understood as a set of principles or practices that, if not present, would make forgiveness impossible.[119] Rather, I have been trying to find a way to affirm the possibility of forgiveness that goes even beyond these understandings to explore where they might lead us. Forgiveness surprises not only because we don't expect it at a certain time or place but because it can be discovered where we think it should not appear when certain circumstances or conditions are present or not.

One might conclude in a given situation that forgiveness simply isn't possible or perhaps even desirable. Nevertheless, it may still emerge and be welcomed like a flower in winter, full of hope and promise and redemption. This is an understanding of forgiveness on this side of complexity that can still embrace the simple mystery of unexpected grace.

Though I am part of an Anabaptist community that stands within the peace tradition of a particular Abrahamic faith, I haven't set out primarily to argue for forgiveness as a requisite Christian principle in need of more regular application, a desired attitude or virtue (or even practice) to be developed, or an ideal outcome to be pursued in every instance of conflict. Though each of these has its rightful place, too often such prescriptions are part of the problem of forgiveness when well-intended counselors, clergy, mediators, friends, and family members fail to recognize the important ways that forgiveness' many factors come together.

When confronted with brokenness, we can't always know what's right or best to do in a given situation or how to forgive or even see what's possible. Perhaps Frederick Buechner put it best:

> There is no book to look up the answer in. There is only your own heart and whatever by God's grace it has picked up in the way of insight, honesty, courage, humility, and, maybe above all else, compassion.[120]

Like healing and reconciliation, I see forgiveness as a gift to be discovered where it emerges—sometimes unexpectedly but almost always with great effort—from life's most painful experiences. My hope is that this short volume has helped you to know what to look for and how to nurture it where it is found.

# NOTES

1. In personal conversation, my colleague Tim Geddert shared that theologian I. Howard Marshall reportedly said something akin to this in a class once, presumably about some complex aspect of the New Testament.

2. These concepts are explored in more detail from a pastoral care perspective in John Patton, *Is Human Forgiveness Possible?* (Nashville: Abingdon Press, 1985); and David W. Augsburger, *Helping People Forgive* (Louisville: Westminster John Know Press, 1996).

3. L. Gregory Jones, *Embodying Forgiveness: A Theological Analysis* (Grand Rapids: Wm. B. Eerdmans Publishing Co., 1995), 37.

4. See *Rich Christians in an Age of Hunger* (Nashville: Thomas Nelson, 2005), first published in 1978 and now in its fifth edition, for the work in mind here.

5. In the article "Needed: A Few More Scholars/Popularizers/Activists: Personal Reflections on my Journey," *Christian Scholar's Review* 36.2 (Winter 2007): 159-166.

6. From "To Smile Again, As Children," CBC Radio. Cited from stjohns.cbc.ca/innuabuse accessed on 9/5/2001.

7. In chapter 9 of *Conflict Mediation Across Cultures* (Louisville: Westminster/John Knox Press, 1992) David Augsburger identifies what he calls the "many faces of forgiveness" from a multi-cultural perspective.

8. On public apologies, see Neil Funk-Unrau, "Renegotiation of Social Relations Through Public Apologies to Canadian Aboriginal Peoples," in *Pushing the Boundaries: New Frontiers in Conflict Resolution and Collaboration Research in Social Movements, Conflicts and Change*, vol. 29, 1-19. For more on apologies and forgiveness in

politics, see Donald W. Shriver Jr., *An Ethic For Enemies: Forgiveness in Politics* (New York: Oxford University Press, 1995).

9. In her book, *Confronting the Horror: The Aftermath of Violence* (Winnipeg: Amity Publishers, 2002) Wilma L. Derksen identifies eleven different kinds of forgiveness. These are not so much exclusive types as they are an identification of the different goals and motivations of forgiveness. See pp. 218-222.

10. See an exploration of metaphor in relation to reconciliation in John Paul Lederach and Angela Jill Lederach, *When Blood and Bones Cry Out: Journeys Through the Soundscape of Healing* (St. Lucia, Qld: University of Queensland Press, 2010), particularly in chapters 1 and 6.

11. The use of the word *like* in this exercise employs the rhetorical device of a simile in which the comparison conveys *some* attributes of the known object to the unknown rather than the equation of one to the other provided by a metaphor (e.g., Fernando is a lion). However, metaphor is used here as the broader term of which all similes are a part.

12. Though not presented in the context of forgiveness, the idea for this metaphor comes from a John Paul Lederach lecture at the twentieth anniversary celebration of the Program on the Analysis and Resolution of Conflicts (PARC) held in 2007 at Syracuse University, available online at www.maxwell.syr.edu/parc. Using a Tibetan singing bowl, Lederach invited the participants to reflect on their own experiences and ideas in relation to the sound metaphor. I attempt that here. For further elaboration of this metaphor in relation to reconciliation, see his book with Angela Jill Lederach, *When Blood and Bones Cry Out: Journeys Through the Soundscape of Healing* (St. Lucia, Qld: University of Queensland Press, 2010).

13. Or other things experienced with our senses, such as smells.

14. Perhaps that's what Bono, U2's lead singer and poet, means in the song "Breathe" when he sings of finding "grace inside a sound." Using this metaphor elsewhere, Bono writes of Judas' "waves of regret" and of "waves of joy" when encountering the forgiveness of a Jesus whom he thought was too preoccupied with the end of the world.

15. In his book, *Lament for a Son* ( London: SPCK, 1997), Nicholas Wolterstorff speaks of how he comes to understand the present suffering brought about by his son's death as experienced directly in proportion to his past (though surely ongoing) love for him. "Some do not suffer much, though, for they do not love much. Suffering is for the loving. If I hadn't loved him, there wouldn't be this agony," 89.

16. In *The Faces of Forgiveness: Searching for Wholeness and Salvation* (Grand Rapids: Baker Academic, 2003), F. LeRon Shults and Steven J. Sandage helpfully identify the roots of this defini-

tional problem by proposing a "conceptual taxonomy for delineating and linking the semantic domains in which the idea of forgiveness operates as a concept," 20. They suggest that our understanding of forgiveness engages three "fields of meaning": the forensic, therapeutic, and redemptive. For our purposes, these categories help us to understand that our experience of forgiveness is broadly shaped by legal, psychological/emotional, and theological/moral concerns which, though unintended, may correspond to aspects of the relational, personal, and cultural "problems" respectively as identified in this chapter.

17. David Augsburger, *Conflict Mediation Across Cultures* (Louisville, Kentucky: Westminster/John Knox Press, 1992), 17.

18. Donald B. Kraybill, Steven M. Nolt, and David L. Weaver-Zercher, *Amish Grace: How Forgiveness Transcended Tragedy* (San Francisco: Jossey-Bass, 2007).

19. Story adapted from original found at The Forgiveness Project website, published on January 27, 2014, http://theforgivenessproject.com/stories/jean-paul-samputu-rwanda/ accessed September 26, 2014.

20. Summarized from *Saint Maybe* by Anne Tyler (New York: Alfred A. Knopf, 1991), 115-124.

21. This insight comes from a lecture by John Paul Lederach at the 2007 Program for the Advancement of Research on Conflict and Collaboration Alumni Conference at Syracuse University (available at http://www.maxwell.syr.edu/parcc/Publications/Videos).

22. This last phrase from a sermon by Bill Braun, pastor of Clovis College Community Church Mennonite Brethren, April 12, 2009.

23. Carol Tavris, *Anger: The Misunderstood Emotion* (New York: Simon & Schuster, 1989).

24. I first came across this distinction in Ron Kraybill's helpful article, "From Head to Heart: The Cycle of Reconciliation." The pathway developed here has come from years of reflection on Kraybill's original article and integration of it with other ideas. *Conciliation Quarterly* (Fall 1988): 2-3, 8.

25. Although, it is only possible *because* of the other and, as Volf argues, we should forgive primarily for other's sake, not our own. See Miroslav Volf, *Free of Charge: Giving and Forgiving in a Culture Stripped of Grace* (Grand Rapids: Zondervan, 2005), 168.

26. A good example of the lingering effects of an unrighteous past, always just under the surface no matter how far removed, is seen in the character of William Munny depicted in Clint Eastwood's 1992 film *Unforgiven*.

27. Psychologists call this the "fundamental attribution error."

28. John Patton, *Is Human Forgiveness Possible?* (Nashville: Abingdon Press, 1985), 16.

29. The story for this introduction and the conclusion below is

taken from CBS, "60 Minutes," March 8, 2009, and at http://www.cbsnews.com/video/watch/?id=4852659n, accessed March 8, 2009; and National Public Radio, "All Things Considered," March 5, 2009, and at http://www.npr.org/templates/story/story.php?storyId=101469307 accessed March 8, 2009.

30. During the period of this project's writing, I have heard apologies from such public figures as Bernard Madoff in expressing remorse for conducting a twenty-year, $65 billion ponzi scheme, golfer Tiger Woods for his deception of both family and fans, and a Japanese official at the crippled Fukushima nuclear power plant, among others. How people responded to disgraced cyclist Lance Armstrong's confession to doping that *lacked* an apology to those he deceived and sought to injure is also instructional.

31. This is Nick Smith's view in his book *I Was Wrong: The Meanings of Apologies* (Cambridge: Cambridge University Press, 2008).

32. Some believe it not appropriate or even possible to apologize ahead of time. They believe it better to use words indicating regret in order to emphasize the importance of "intent to change" in the meaning of apology. However, I can imagine that one could genuinely apologize for needing to make a forced choice or for the anticipated undesirable consequences of such a choice. More will be said about this later.

33. John Paul Lederach, *Preparing for Peace* (Syracuse: Syracuse University Press, 1985), 8-9.

34. Edward C. Valandra, "Decolonizing 'Truth': Restoring More than Justice," 29-53, in *Justice as Healing: Indigenous Ways*, ed. Wanda D. McCaslin (St. Paul: Living Justice Press, 2005).

35. The importance of the order of this seems unclear. For example, on learning of a harm committed against another, one might grimace and verbally respond with "Oh no!" even in the process of hearing from the victim, sending an initial signal of regret and intent to make the situation right.

36. David Augsburger, *Helping People Forgive* (Louisville: Westminster John Knox Press, 1996), 39.

37. Nicholas Tavuchis, *Mea Culpa: A Sociology of Apology and Reconciliation* (Stanford: Stanford University Press, 1991), 8, 23.

38. As cited in David Augsburger, *Conflict Mediation Across Cultures* (Louisville: Westminster/John Knox Press, 1992), 259.

39. By Mike Twohy, *The New Yorker* (September 21, 2009), 46.

40. Such an example occurred in response to one South African apartheid official's request for forgiveness by a family who perceived the request as too late and in his own self interest. The attack on him with a bottle in the family's home was shown in Helen Whitney's 2011 film, *Forgiveness: A Time to Love and A Time to Hate*, part one.

41. From Whitney's *Forgiveness: A Time to Love and A Time to Hate*, part one. Power was eventually released from prison a year-and-a-half later in October of 1999.

42. Ron Kraybill, "From Head to Heart: The Cycle of Reconciliation," *Conciliation Quarterly* (Fall 1988): 8.

43. By Edward Koren, *The New Yorker* (November 21, 1994): 99.

44. Lance Morrow in Helen Whitney's 2011 film, *Forgiveness: A Time to Love and A Time to Hate*, part one.

45. Nicholas Tavuchis, *Mea Culpa: A Sociology of Apology and Reconciliation* (Stanford: Stanford University Press, 1991), 13.

46. "Drabble," by Kevin Fagan (September 14, 2009).

47. From Helen Whitney's 2011 film, *Forgiveness: A Time to Love and A Time to Hate*, part one.

48. John Patton, *Is Human Forgiveness Possible?* (Nashville: Abingdon Press, 1985), 83.

49. There are, of course, many analyses of the TRC process from a variety of perspectives. Even though it was central to the process, one perspective is that the TRC was not best understood as the ideal forum for individual acts of reconciliation, however powerful its rare occurrence was; rather, the TRC is best thought of as having provided a symbolic venue for a nation coming to terms with what it did to itself as a whole. See Helen Whitney's *Forgiveness: A Time to Love and A Time to Hate*, (2011) part two.

50. From a personal conversation with Mary Anne Isaac, pastor of Clovis (Calif.) College Community Church Mennonite Brethren.

51. C. Norman Kraus, *The Jesus Factor in Justice and Peacemaking* (Telford, Pa.: Cascadia Publishing House, 2011), 83.

52. Frederick Buechner, *Whistling in the Dark: An ABC Theologized* (San Francisco: Harper & Row, 1988), 68.

53. Robert McAfee Brown notes the "revenge" of Tomas Borge, a Nicaraguan Sandinista fighter entitled by the court at his torturer's trial to name the appropriate punishment: "My punishment," he said, "is to forgive you." In *The Sunflower: On the Possibilities and Limits of Forgiveness*, ed Simon Wiesenthal (New York: Schocken Books, 1997), 123.

54. The Rev. James Forbes, in *The Power of Forgiveness*, by Martin Doblemeier, Journey Films, 2008.

55. Frederich Buechner suggests that the unconditional nature of forgiveness is the reason why Jesus' prayer, "Forgive us our trespasses as we forgive those who trespass against us," does *not* mean that we are only forgiven by God to the same degree that we forgive others. In fact, he says that our unforgiving-ness "is among those things about us which we need to have God forgive us most." The real meaning of Jesus' prayer, he suggests, might just be that "the pride which keeps us from forgiving is the same pride which keeps us from accepting forgiveness, and will God please help us

do something about it." *Wishful Thinking: A Theological ABC* (San Francisco: Harper & Row, 1973), 29.

56. Jacques Derrida, *On Cosmopolitanism and Forgiveness* (London: Routledge, 2001), 36.

57. See Elie Wiesel, *From the Kingdom of Memory: Reminiscences* (New York: Schocken Books, 1990); and *Conversations with Elie Wiesel,* Elie Wiesel and Richard D. Heffner (New York: Schocken Books, 2001), especially ch. 11, "The Mystic Chords of Memory."

58. Zeljiko Vukovic, *The Killing of Sarajevo* (Belgrade: Kron, 1993), 134 as found in David Augsburger's *Hate-Work: Working Through the Pain and Pleasures of Hate* (Louisville: Westminster John Knox Press, 2004), 73.

59. Miroslav Volf, *The End of Memory: Remembering Rightly in a Violent World* (Grand Rapids: William B. Eerdmans Publishing Company, 2006), 11.

60. John Patton, *Is Human Forgiveness Possible?* (Nashville: Abingdon Press, 1985), 14. Miroslav Volf also makes an important and relevant distinction between those claiming to *possess* the truth and those committed to seeking the *truth,* in *The End of Memory: Remembering Rightly in a Violent World* (Grand Rapids: William B. Eerdmans Publishing Company, 2006), 57. See also John Paul Lederach's reflection on the important role of truth, mercy, justice, and peace in relation to reconciliation in *The Journey Toward Reconciliation* (Scottdale, Pa.: Herald Press, 1999), chapter four.

61. Miroslav Volf, *The End of Memory: Remembering Rightly in a Violent World* (Grand Rapids: William B. Eerdmans Publishing Company, 2006), 55.

62. David Augsburger, *Hate-Work: Working Through the Pain and Pleasures of Hate* (Louisville: Westminster John Knox Press, 2004), 77.

63. This is true for both victim and offender. Buechner suggests that being remembered keeps us from becoming lost, helps serve as a reminder that we actually exist. See *Whistling in the Dark: An ABC Theologized* (San Francisco: Harper & Row, 1988), 100.

64. Mohandas K. Gandhi, *An Autobiography: The Story of My Experiments with Truth* (Boston: Beacon Press, 1993), xvii and 276 where he quotes the rarely practiced precept "hate the sin and not the sinner." See also St. Augustine's *Cum dilectione hominum et odio vitiorum* ("With love for mankind and hatred of sins"), Opera Omnia, vol II. col. 962, letter 211.

65. Miroslav Volf, *Free of Charge: Giving and Forgiving in a Culture Stripped of Grace* (Grand Rapids: Zondervan, 2005), 175.

66. *Dissent* interview with Avishai Margalit (http://www.dissentmagazine.org/online.php?id=37) accessed on July 24, 2009.

67. Louis Kriesberg and Bruce W. Dayton, *Constructive Conflicts: From Escalation to Resolution,* 4th. ed. (Lanham: Rowman &

Littlefield Publishers, Inc., 2012), 306.

68. Miroslav Volf, *Exclusion and Embrace: A Theological Exploration of Identity, Otherness, and Reconciliation* (Nashville: Abingdon Press, 1996), 131.

69. Miroslav Volf, *Exclusion and Embrace: A Theological Exploration of Identity, Otherness, and Reconciliation* (Nashville: Abingdon Press, 1996), 131.

70. Miroslav Volf, *The End of Memory: Remembering Rightly in a Violent World* (Grand Rapids: William B. Eerdmans Publishing Company, 2006), 83.

71. Frederick Buechner, *Wishful Thinking: A Theological ABC* (San Francisco: Harper & Row, 1973), 28-29.

72. Ray S. Anderson suggests that "Love's great power to heal through forgiveness is matched only by its power to destroy through reaction to betrayal." In *The Gospel According to Judas* (Colorado Springs: Helmers & Howard, 1991), 14.

73. Martin Doblemeier's 2007 film "The Power of Forgiveness."

74. Didier Pollefeyt, "Ethics, Forgiveness and the Unforgivable After Auschwitz," 121-159 in *Incredible Forgiveness: Christian Ethics between Fanaticism and Reconciliation*, ed. Didier Pollefeyt (Leuven-Dudley: Peeters, 2004), 122.

75. Alasdair MacIntyre, *After Virtue* (Notre Dame, Indiana: University of Notre Dame Press, 1984), 187.

76. MacIntyre, *After Virtue*, 193, 191.

77. Glen H. Stassen, *Living the Sermon on the Mount: A Practical Hope for Grace and Deliverance*, (San Francisco: John Wiley & Sons, Inc., 2006), 16.

78. Donald B. Kraybill, Steven M. Nolt, and David L. Weaver-Zercher, *Amish Grace: How Forgiveness Transcended Tragedy* (San Francisco: Jossey-Bass, 2007), 140.

79. Kraybill, Nolt, and Weaver-Zercher, 140.

80. Kraybill, Nolt, and Weaver-Zercher, 68.

81. Kraybill, Nolt, and Weaver-Zercher, 140.

82. Celestin Musekura, *An Assessment of Contemporary Models of Forgiveness*, American University Studies VII: Theology and Religion, vol. 302 (New York: Peter Lang, 2010), 116-117.

83. Musekura addresses the challenges of political forgiveness in his chapter, "Communal Forgiveness: A Multifaceted Model." *An Assessment of Contemporary Models of Forgiveness*, American University Studies VII: Theology and Religion, vol. 302 (New York: Peter Lang, 2010), 137-188.

84. See Larry A. Dunn, "Transforming Identity in Conflict," in *Making Peace with Conflict*, ed. Carolyn Schrock-Shenk and Lawrence Ressler (Scottdale, Pa.: Herald Press, 1999), 45. The Stanley Hauerwas quote comes from "The Church's One Foundation is Jesus Christ Her Lord; Or, In a World Without

Foundations: All We Have is the Church," in *Theology Without Foundations: Religious Practice and the Future of Theological Truth*, ed. Nancy Murphy, Mark Nation, and Stanley Hauerwas (Nashville: Abingdon Press, 1994), 157.

85. Etienne Wenger, *Communities of Practice: Learning, Meaning, and Identity* (Cambridge, England: Cambridge University Press, 1998).

86. I first encountered a version of this story as rewritten in shortened parable form by David Augsburger in his book *Helping People Forgive* (Louisville: Westminster John Knox Press, 1996), 103. I am indebted to Augsburger for helping me to shape this version of my own. I have drawn primarily from the much longer original as written by Max Beerbohm, *The Happy Hypocrite: A Fairy Tale for Tired Men* originally published in Great Britain (Edinburgh: Turnbull & Spears, 1897) and now available for free on The Project Gutenberg web site (http://www.gutenberg.org/files/36497/36497-h/36497-h.htm), accessed on September 4, 2014.

87. Augsburger, *Helping People Forgive*, 103.

88. As noted by Gandhi's grandson, Arun Gandhi, "Forward: My Grandfather's Footsteps," in *In the Footsteps of Gandhi: Conversations with Spiritual Social Activists* (Berkeley: Parallax Press, 2003), 11.

89. This concept was first introduced to me as a University Graduate Fellow and Teaching Assistant at Syracuse University in a class taught by Neil Katz. It is based on a learning model first developed by Noel Burch at Gordon Training International. I have summarized the model here referencing an overview of the process as described by GTI President Linda Adams, http://www.gordon-training.com/free-workplace-articles/learning-a-new-skill-is-easier-said-than-done/, accessed on September 4, 2014.

90. Lederach calls such pessimism "a luxurious avoidance of engagement," *The Moral Imagination: The Art and Soul of Building Peace* (Oxford: Oxford University Press, 2005), 55.

91. Martin Luther King Jr., *Strength to Love* (New York: Harper & Row, 1963), 1.

92. John Paul Lederach, *The Moral Imagination: The Art and Soul of Building Peace* (Oxford: Oxford University Press, 2005), 61.

93. I don't doubt that, inclusive of the possibility of forgiveness, reconciliation may be even more complex than forgiveness since by definition it requires the involvement of two or more parties. As C. Norman Kraus notes in his book, *The Jesus Factor in Justice and Peacemaking* (Telford, Pa.: Cascadia Publishing House, 2011), reconciliation not only "includes the healing of alienation and the restoration of respect and trust," but it is also "more than re-balancing power relationships, satisfying the victim's need for 'closure,' or the therapeutic rehabilitation of the offender" (pp. 61-62.), each

involved processes of their own.

94. The use of the term *problem* is certainly not intended to argue *against* forgiveness or suggest its impossibility. Rather, it is meant to identify difficult issues that emerge in a variety of situations of offense where forgiveness is considered. No list, including this one, can be exhaustive.

95. F. LeRon Shults and Steven J. Sandage explore what they call the intersubjective characterological dispositions toward forgiveness and unforgiveness in part 1 of their book *The Faces of Forgiveness: Searching for Wholeness and Salvation* (Grand Rapids: Baker Academic, 2003).

96. John Patton, *Is Human Forgiveness Possible?* (Nashville: Abingdon Press, 1985).

97. David Augsburger, *Pastoral Counseling Across Cultures* (Philadelphia: The Westminster Press, 1986), 115. Augsburger's lengthier chapter on both guilt and shame are helpful for understanding the distinctions between them and both their positive and negative sides, particularly from a cross-cultural perspective. See ch. 4, "Inner Controls, Outer Controls, Balanced Controls: A Theology of Grace," 111-143.

98. Ray S. Anderson, *The Gospel According to Judas* (Colorado Springs: Helmers & Howard, 1991), 37. Anderson depicts a tormented Judas confronting a forgiving Jesus: "Don't you realize that for the betrayer, love is a cruel reminder of failure? Go away! I have enough pain without your love punishing me further," 7- 8.

99. David Augsburger, *Pastoral Counseling Across Cultures* (Philadelphia: The Westminster Press, 1986), 118.

100. Robert Coles, in *The Sunflower: On the Possibilities and Limits of Forgiveness*, ed. Simon Wiesenthal (New York: Schocken Books, 1997), 128.

101. David Augsburger, *Pastoral Counseling Across Cultures* (Philadelphia: The Westminster Press, 1986), 113.

102. Martin Doblemeier's 2007 film "The Power of Forgiveness" documents a number of contexts in which people are working to overcome such memories and the control they exert over the present.

103. Jacques Derrida, *On Cosmopolitanism and Forgiveness* (London: Routledge, 2001), 31.

104. David W. Augsburger, *Conflict Mediation Across Cultures* (Louisville: Westminster/John Knox Press, 1992), ch. 9.

105. Nechama Tec, in *The Sunflower: On the Possibilities and Limits of Forgiveness*, ed. Simon Wiesenthal (New York: Schocken Books, 1997), 261.

106. David Augsburger, *Helping People Forgive* (Louisville: Westminster John Knox Press, 1996), 6.

107. C. Norman Kraus, *The Jesus Factor in Justice and Peacemaking*

(Telford, Pennsylvania: Cascadia Publishing House, 2011), 60- 61.

108. Kraus, *The Jesus Factor in Justice and Peacemaking*, 83 (italics his).

109. Martin Luther King, Jr. *Strength to Love* (New York: Harper & Row, 1963), 35.

110. John Paul Lederach and Angela Jill Lederach, *When Blood and Bones Cry Out: Journeys Through the Soundscape of Healing* (St. Lucia, Qld: University of Queensland Press, 2010).

111. Alasdair MacIntyre, *After Virtue* (Notre Dame, Indiana: University of Notre Dame Press, 1984), 171, 174, 187.

112. Desmond Tutu, *No Future Without Forgiveness* (New York: Doubleday, 1999).

113. In his book, *Forgiveness: A Philosophical Exploration* (Cambridge: Cambridge University Press, 2007), Charles L. Griswold concurs with this idea, though he makes a distinction between what he calls affirmative reconciliation ("something like friendship and support or a renewal of any previous ties of affection") to which this notion applies and reconciliation as acceptance ("the minimal sense of non-interference") to which it does not. Interpersonal forgiveness, he says, is a necessary condition of the former, but not the latter. Having made this distinction, Griswold argues that affirmative reconciliation is neither a necessary nor appropriate political goal (111) underscoring Louis Kriesberg's and Bruce W. Dayton's point that neither is reconciliation "an inevitable stage in every conflict," 308. See *Constructive Conflicts: From Escalation to Resolution*, 4th. ed. (Lanham: Rowman & Littlefield Publishers, Inc., 2012).

114. John Paul Lederach, *The Moral Imagination: The Art and Soul of Building Peace* (Oxford: Oxford University Press, 2005), 44.

115. As noted above, John Paul Lederach reflects on the role of truth, mercy, justice and peace in relation to reconciliation in *The Journey Toward Reconciliation* (Scottdale, Pa.: Herald Press, 1999). Louis Kriesberg and Bruce W. Dayton address additional aspects of these concerns, characterizing Lederach's forces as aspects of reconciliation: truth, justice, regard, and security. See *Constructive Conflicts: From Escalation to Resolution*, 4th. ed.(Lanham: Rowman & Littlefield Publishers, Inc., 2012), 304-9.

116. The story is recounted, among other places, in Tony Campolo's *Let Me Tell You a Story* (Nashville: Thomas Nelson, 2000). Various accounts report different contexts for Barth's response.

117. John Paul Lederach, *The Moral Imagination: The Art and Soul of Building Peace* (Oxford: Oxford University Press, 2005), 33.

118. Lederach, *The Moral Imagination*, 34.

119. This is how Lederach describes what he calls the "core" set of disciplines or practices of peacebuilding. I don't mean to suggest that it is not helpful for him or for us to think this way.

120. Frederick Buechner, *Whistling in the Dark: An ABC Theologized* (San Francisco: Harper & Row, 1988), 74.

# THE AUTHOR

Larry Dunn has worked for nearly thirty years as a mediator, trainer, consultant and educator in the field of conflict resolution. He is currently an associate professor in the School of Humanities, Religion, and Social Sciences at the Center for Peacemaking and Conflict Studies at Fresno Pacific University.

Dunn holds a Masters degree in Theology from Fuller Theological Seminary and a PhD in Social Science from Syracuse University, where he was affiliated with the Program on the Analysis and Resolution of Conflicts. From 1997-99 Dunn served with the Mennonite Central Committee in Labrador (Canada) as a cross-cultural conflict consultant working with Aboriginal communities and First Nations on community justice, self-government and land rights issues.

Dunn has mediated a wide variety of cases involving neighbors, families, schools, churches, businesses, communities, and government agencies. He has published articles and chapters on topics ranging from church disputes to international mediation and ethnic conflict.

Dunn and his wife Susan have three boys, Seth (now deceased), Eli, and Isaac, and are members of College Community Church Mennonite Brethren in Clovis, California.

CPSIA information can be obtained
at www.ICGtesting.com
Printed in the USA
FSHW011709010919
61525FS